# AN ILFORD BOYHOOD

*Early twenties solid tyred omnibus, aptly nicknamed "bone shakers".*
*The entire route was on stone setts!*
*(Photograph by courtesy of Local History Library, Redbridge)*

*Mother and twins (Me standing). Spring, 1925*

# AN ILFORD BOYHOOD

# PETER FORD

IAN HENRY PUBLICATIONS

DEDICATED TO THE MEMORY
of my dearest friend, Anthony
and his twin sister,
who, with Twin and I
shared so many experiences
between the wars.

British Library Cataloguing in Publication Data
Ford, Peter
   An Ilford boyhood
   1. London (England). Social life. History. 1918-1939
   I. Title
   942.173

   ISBN 0-86025-440-2

*The cover photograph is of Ilford Broadway in 1926*
*(Photograph by courtesy of Local History Library, Redbridge)*

Printed by
Ennisfield Print & Design
6/8 The Highway, London E1 9BQ
for
Ian Henry Publications, Ltd.,
20 Park Drive, Romford, Essex RM1 4LH

# INTRODUCTION

When researching for my book *Tendring Peninsula: Land of Milk and Hunnye* I became increasingly aware of the many social changes occurring throughout the short span of our personal history and how changes often mushroomed after major events, such as wars, thus breaking away from any gentle evolutionary curve on the historical graph.

Between World Wars One and Two it seems to me we see enormous movements in social habits, ethics, morality, religion, conventions, education and technology; those of us who grew up in these years no doubt accept it as normal progress of civilised humanity – until, that is, our children's children say, "Was it really like that when you were a little boy, Grandpa?" Then they add, after the goodnight kiss, "Promise to tell us more next time we come."

That family request motivated this recollection of life between the wars in the expanding suburbs of London. I offer it as a 'word photograph' of bygones with inevitable distortions through the fading of time and necessarily selective anecdotes of nostalgic experiences of the 1920s.

For the mature, my it evoke fascinating memories; for the young, satisfy curiosity and, hopefully, maybe, help establish an even deeper appreciation of our heritage as it has evolved.

P.C.F.
Frinton, 1991

*Mother's family. Mother 2nd from left, back row. "Pessary aunt" extreme right. All blouses made by each member*

# EARLY DAYS

*Pop goes the weasel* in Father's clear baritone is my first childhood memory. He sang this every morning at 57 Sandyhill Road, Ilford, when lighting the gas lamp over my cot in the bedroom I shared with my twin sister and parents in the early 1920s. As the gas flickered, popped and strengthened I could see Twin standing in her cot staring large-eyed over the rail, seemingly wondering why I was grizzling. Normally a contented child, unlike me, she rarely cried.

"I'll do the boy, Laurie, otherwise he'll go on making a fuss, and you can do the girl," said Mother from the brass bedstead.

This *doing* was a changing of nappies with the inevitable plop as they were dropped into an enamelled bucket and a satisfying clang of the lid before Father clumped downstairs to place them in soak. He wore an ankle length plaid dressing gown, essential against the grim dankness of the house until the sole heating from the dining room fire began to cheer us after breakfast.

Mother remained in bed for her early morning tea and biscuit and seemed to me like a stranger in her knitted shawl and without her pince-nez. Only the better-off had warm bedrooms; the rest of us awoke to cold noses in various hues.

Another memory from before the age of speech is being in bed with Mother during a devastating influenza epidemic when a booming-voiced doctor demanded a teaspoon to hold down my tongue to peer down my throat before using it to investigate Mother's. During this ordeal and as I screamed, Mother cuddled me, but seemed strangely hot, sticky and worried as she asked weakly, "Is the girl alright?"

For several years we were not spoken of or to

3

by name: it was either *the boy* or *the girl* and, if together, *the twins* or, when being addressed *you two*. On reaching an age of more discretion, which in our case meant when we were cunning enough to overhear adult conversations secretly, an occupation at which my twin excelled behind the settee, we learnt that nobody had realised that our poor mother, married at 22 years of age, was carrying twins until *the girl* was actually born and, Grandmama, an ex-nursing sister, then shouted to the doctor, "Wait a minute, there's another one coming!" We also heard from behind the settee that *the boy* had to be delivered by forceps and poor Annie *lost so much* she would always be *anaemic*. In our muddled childish way we thought this was a grown-up name for Mother, only to be used when we were out of the way. We felt slightly guilty at such a name change.

We also learnt on the knowledge-gathering-circuit that children use in the field of human understanding that Mother, being the youngest but one and first married of five sisters had to be looked after, advised, interfered with, exhorted and bossed about, especially by her eldest sister, who soon alienated me from any nephew-based affection by insisting on inserting a carefully-shaped Lifebuoy soap pessary into my offended posterior whilst I was contemplating the dining room fire from the comfort and security (so I thought) of a chamber pot.

At that time I had no idea what constipation was; we were soon to dread the word, as it described a family obsession (typical of the times) and all female relatives had their own pet remedies, all of which were used on us: soap pessaries, senna pods and castor oil were the worst; California Syrup of Figs nearly as bad; and liquid paraffin just bearable. By the age of six we learnt to answer a firm 'Yes' to the question, 'Have you been today?'. Subsequently only once did we answer 'no', when a wealthy

4

*Some two-holers came in one size, others catered for different age groups (Photographed at the Museum of East Anglian Life, Stowmarket)*

*Mother's eldest sister, Nora (Soap Pessary expert) with the twins in Sandyhill Road, 1923*

American aunt came to stay and showed us her tempting packets of laxative chocolates she was pleased to administer in small pieces. Drastic results cured us of that particular lie.

Our terrace house lavatory was in the yard and sported a scrubbed wooden seat, far more warm and comfortable than modern plastic and it also supported a generous wooden surround as waiting space. We chatted happily in that private and rarely invaded refuge of obligation. Friends in more prestigious houses in the country had double seats, some even equipped with lower level seats for infants.

In the scullery was a solitary cold water tap above the 9 inch deep earthenware sink, hot water came from a kettle heated in winter on the dining room fire and in summer on the gas stove. Housework was hard and continuous: Monday was wash-day when water had to be heated in a gas-fired tub. A wooden handled perforated copper cone (posser) was used to agitate clothes in soapy water, then a scrubbing board of rippled galvanised sheet steel was inserted and with bare hands rapidly becoming red and puffy and, eventually, white and wrinkled, Mother rubbed each garment vigorously and often viciously.

All soap work had to be done first and each article wrung through the cumbersome wooden-rollered mangle; then a break for her cup of tea, whilst the tub was re-heating for rinsing water. Finally, sheets, tablecloths and serviettes (never called 'napkins' in our circles) were treated to bluing in cold water with a Reckitt's blue dolly bag, complete with string for dunking. Too much and they turned grey, just enough and the slight blue tint was supposed to enhance whiteness. A bowl of Robin Starch was maturing in the meantime and collars, table linen, shirt cuffs and dressing table mats were immersed and then mangled and added to the huge pile of damp material. By this time it would be mid-day and in-

6

variably cold meat and mashed potatoes with home-made chutney. While potatoes were cooking, washing was hung on the line in good weather or, in bad, festooned over airers in front of the fire or hung from the scullery ceiling on a pulley and rope contraption. Soon the whole house dripped with condensation, but with a clean, soapy smell.

Tuesday was ironing day. Mother had two solid irons which she heated in front of the fire or on a gas ring; the ironing board was the dining room table covered with heat stained woollen blankets and topped with doubled-over scorch-blotched linen or cotton sheets honourably retired from long bedroom service. Looking back, life was physically hard for mothers, but at least they were largely free from a modern tendency to denigrate the occupation of housewife in favour of careers. Not surprisingly, the best time to ask Mother any favours in the way of sweets was last thing Tuesday evening, when the ironing was neatly folded and stacked.

Although domestic labour-saving devices were scarce, it was easy to hire help, if money was avail-able; it was in our case, as Father was Manager of the calendar department in a large printing company, earning £4 a week from which in five years he paid back the £300 he had borrowed from Grandpa to buy the house: this was a grim struggle and spurred his decision to attend evening classes for a qualification which enabled him to lecture for the London County Council several evenings a week. He told me towards the end of his life that in those early days, with an unexpected extra mouth to feed, he often felt desperate and thus compelled to work every hour he could to keep out of debt - everybody's dread in those slump-ridden days.

By the time we were five years old he was handling the advertising as a free-lance for Harrison Gibson's, Smith Motors and Essex Water Softeners, hoping one day to be big enough to leave the printers and become self-employed. Whilst holding down these two jobs, he was also teaching himself New Testament Greek and Hebrew. When it was Mother's turn to go to church, he would sit us one on each knee and chant from Hebrew and Greek grammars held open between us. The guttural parrot-fashion learning was soporific and we had the doubtful distinction of being lullabied in Biblical languages.

I sometimes wonder how many autodidacts have been appointed to teach Biblical languages, as Father was and did for seven years at Rochester Theological College when 64 years of age and retired from his own engineering business.

Two pram memories are still clear: the first is of being in our 'twins fore and aft hooded pram' on the front path at 57 Sandyhill Road, and I can recall biting my sister's thumb until her screams brought Father from behind his Greek. I was smacked hard and, in my anger and pain, bounced up and down to such effect that the pram tilted forward as we swung dangerously from our seat belts. Father's consternation seemed to ease my pain! Corporal punishment was meted out on all ages and I cannot recall any public opprobrium, nor do I think it did me any harm!

The other memory is of a rainy day in Ilford Lane, near the Broadway, when Mother stopped to talk to a friend as we pushed our fingers through the gap between hoods to enjoy a syrupy female voice saying, "Look at them twins wrigglin' their fingers - the little darlin's." How satisfying it was to be noticed! I'm sure there were just as many twins then as now, but we certainly gained the impression we were special; perhaps in Ilford in those days twins were rare.

On reflection it is interesting to know that understanding of language seems to come long before speech. Conversely, the frustration of not being able

8

to make adults understand lurks in my memory in one incident in Ilford High Road, outside the Penny Bazaar, near The Broadway; this brightly-gas-lit store had balloons tethered over the entrance and I clearly, so I thought, said to an aunt holding my hand, "I want a balloon." She asked me to repeat the request, which I did several times, only to reduce her to helpless giggles, as she dragged me on to a tram. I have never discovered what she thought I had said, but the bitter disappointment consequent upon inadequate powers of communication remained with me for a number of years.

Many decades later, an elderly stroke victim told me that before he recovered, whenever he tried to speak, only rubbish noises came out; his frustration turned to anger and even recalling those painful emotions made him feel ill years later. He also said it had provided him with an incentive to persevere with speech therapy. Perhaps, as infants, learning to speak is similarly motivated. My twin and I, however, communicated by sound long before adults could comprehend a word we said, except, that is, for Lena, who was Mother's first helper in the house and could always be appealed to by adults for translations of our language. This skill may have accelerated the termination of her employment, as Mother resented her understanding of and special influence on the twins. We loved her dearly and were devastated when she failed to appear the morning after a tearful scene we overheard at bedtime between our parents, with Mother saying, whilst sobbing hysterically, "She'll have to go, Laurie, I can't **stand** it any longer!" In our inchoate understanding of adult emotions and motives we sensed Mother's jealousy and insecurity and somehow this made us feel guilty for loving and being able to communicate with our dear Lena.

Thereafter domestic help was notable more for frequent changes than for efficiency and personal

9

relationships. As we grew up and began to debate these things we concluded, rightly or wrongly, that Mother had a complex about employing people as she was always aware of being a shopkeeper's daughter and not quite **up to** employing anybody herself.

Nevertheless, Mother was very happy in Sandyhill Road, which must have seemed like heaven after sharing our birthplace, 19 Bedford Road, Ilford, with a newly married couple, buying that solidly-built Edwardian terrace house on borrowed money and anxious to clear the debt as soon as possible by letting rooms. The house was not divided into flats; my people had the back bedroom, used the breakfast room as a dining room and sitting room, shared bathroom, lavatory and kitchen and, when we arrived on the scene, had to wipe the wheels of the cumbersome twin pram each time before entering the hall in fair or foul weather.

How Mother managed early married life, pregnancy, childbirth and all subsequent chores in such impossible circumstances is difficult to imagine.

After the Great War it was relatively easy to find somewhere to live in rented accommodation, even if it was sometimes inconvenient or inadequate; at least, young married couples could launch into independence, providing, of course, the husband was in work. Many Ilford widows let the top floors of their house unfurnished and several builders, small traders, and craftsmen bought as many terraced houses as they could afford for their widows to be able to rent out by way of income. One small jobbing builder we knew had five terraced houses in Kingston Road, Ilford, which he left to his widow on his death in 1932: she lived comfortably on the rents.

The ready availability of rented accommodation helped mobility of labour and, in those difficult days when jobs were scarce, enabled many men to move some distance, together with their families, to

10

another job.

In church circles in which we mixed, several widows lived modestly on rental income from part of the house, offering good value in hard, competitive times, in the comforting knowledge that their husbands had provided the most permanent arrangement known to any artisan between the wars, namely, the freehold of bricks and mortar assuring, so they thought, steady rents for the foreseeable future. The Victorian ethos of permanency and security in property and the unchanging value of all material things, still pervading the Ilford of my boyhood was one reason why private property to rent was easily available at all price levels.

Most newly-weds began life as tenants. Some eventually moved to the huge London County Council estates in Becontree and Dagenham, while others bought their own houses from such people as Holmes White Homes at Goodmayes and Chadwell Heath, where prices for new three bedroomed houses began well below £500.

Successive governments since World War II have, in effect, virtually destroyed the facility of renting from private landlords at affordable rents for all pockets and thus indirectly (maybe unintentionally) inflated the cost of living accommodation today; but, when we consider that the really poor, unable to afford even the most modest rent during my boyhood, were virtually without hope, perhaps Welfare State handouts since the last war have compensated somewhat for this vanishing of private landlords under the yoke and restrictions of property laws, initially designed to prevent the escalation of Rachmanism.

Building Societies grew steadily between the wars and veritably mushroomed after World War II as rented property, through bomb damage and material shortages, became scarce. In the 1920s, however, estate agents in Ilford, as elsewhere, could

11

provide lists of flats, shared portions of houses, and many complete homes of any size to rent in any road: it was only the independent minded or those in safe employment who could contemplate shouldering the responsibilities of a mortgage via a Building Society. Safe employment was rare, better a private landlord with a face to appeal to if in trouble, better still a debt to helpful relatives, than to impersonal usurers. Many of our friends and relations bought their houses with private loans from relatives fortunate enough to have modest capital to invest: far preferable to 'falling into the hands' of building societies.

Property values remained fairly constant, but, unlike today, new houses lost value after a few years, not catastrophically, it is true, but to be reckoned with seriously. In 1928 Father bought a new three bedroomed bungalow in Seven Kings for £590 and was glad to receive £470 for it six years later, despite costly improvements, such as garage, concrete drive, sheds and expensive garden features.

We may have been unusual as a family (although I doubt it), but help from relatives rather than financial institutions was the norm. Whenever one of the family was in difficulty, whether financial or moral, through stupidity, misfortune or inadequacy, it was to relatives the first appeal for help was made and invariably from them given. I suspect this was the normal way of life for most people.

Our family circle, both paternal and maternal, have many examples of private enterprises and self-help. Grandpa Collins, Mother's father, humbly born in a seafaring family in Gravesend, began his working life as a shop assistant in a Gentlemen's Outfitter (never Men's Outfitter in those days) in the late 19th century. When his boss died, he and another member of staff bought the business on borrowed money, building up the trade and personal stakes under the name of Sharpe & Collins to the point where Grandpa was able to buy out his older partner and continue in business as Arthur Collins until he died in 1927; by then he had also bought the freehold of the shop and living accommodation. Grandma was able to live on the rent from the tenant who had bought the goodwill and stock of the business, to run it successfully until 1957, much to the benefit of Grandpa's heirs and assigns. All this was achieved after leaving school before the age of 14 and with no family help.

Grandpapa Ford, similarly humbly born, had musical talent. As a lad he left Bedford for work in London where, in his spare time, he associated with a professional church organist, perfecting his innate skills to such effect that he was able to obtain the position of organist and choirmaster at Bunyan Meeting, Bedford, where he also taught music and singing in the chapel, home and local school. In those days practical musical ability was valued, even if without academic qualifications, and titles assumed as of right by virtue of practised skills. On Father's birth certificate Grandpapa's occupation is recorded as Professor of Music and dated July 1st, 1895; similarly my paternal grandmother's father, Francis Thomas Mercer, signed a sketch of Bedford High Street F.T.Mercer Architect. He was well known and practised as an architect in Bedford, his only qualifications appear to have been sheer ability.

After his first wife died, leaving him three sons and two daughters, Grandpapa Ford married Lizzie Duncombe Mercer, who was twenty years his junior. Unlike today, this caused a stir and was frowned upon by all concerned as being very unsuitable and definitely not to be encouraged. It was, in fact, a very happy marriage, producing three more sons and two further daughters. Not surprisingly, money began to dry up with Grandpapa's increasing age and educating his second family became a problem. As so often happened in those days, the eldest son

13

obtained the best and most expensive schooling, while the others gradually decreased in cost until the youngest son in the Ford family was sent to a childless aunt married to the Editor of the *Yorkshire Post* to be educated free of charge to Grandpapa. Education was considered of such vital importance that the trauma of separation from the family for the sake of later advancement was overlooked. Being sent to boarding school was bad enough, but also having to spend holidays away from home was hard.

These days we find it hard to believe how difficult it was to obtain an education leading to a professional qualification if adequate funds were not available. Any opportunity opening up was seized, even if it meant deprivation of loving care in the family bosom. My grandparents suffered awful 'heart-string' pangs sending Father's younger brother into education emigration, but it was for 'his good' according to accepted views of the time. Many years later, Uncle divulged to me, when we were in business together selling dairy machinery, that he still felt resentful at being sent away from home, even though it was beneficial materially and opportunistically.

The two girls of the second family had to take pot luck and were educated mainly at their mother's excellent knee. This stood the family in good stead when Grandpapa died and my grandmother opened a small kindergarten school, with her two girls assisting as unqualified teachers and general factotums. Desperate, rather than private, enterprise, I fear, and eventually doomed to failure.

My only personal memory of Grandpapa Ford (called Papa by his family and nicknamed by himself Pater Family Ass) was of a visit my twin and I paid to Bedford from Ilford when suffering from violent whooping cough at the age of $3\frac{1}{2}$. In those days it was supposed that running water cured this noisy, painful complaint. The River Ouse, although sluggish in

*Grandfather Ford*

*The twins
damming
a small stream
fifteen minutes
walk south from
Levett Gardens,
Seven Kings, 1932*

15

summer, certainly flowed at great speed during rain storms or after thaws and was considered suitable for cures. Free accommodation added attraction.

Elderly Grandpapa walked beside us as Mother pushed our heavy pram along The Embankment. He smelt of rank tobacco (which, from our smoke-free experience, we found strangely exciting) and, between burbling sucks on a sagging pipe, his melodious voice indicated pools where various pike had been taken and subsequently cooked with herbs in a kitchen from which, at such important occasions, females were prohibited. I cannot remember eating pike, but many years later Father told me Papa's pike tasted of herb flavoured earth and had many sharp bone hazards. The family hated pike and the way Papa enthused over every detail of his recipe whilst noisily partaking.

Grandmama Ford never pretended to be a competent cook, which was unusual then; possibly such an early marriage to an experienced family man with a ready made family required a certain amount of discretion (especially with regard to cooking) from a young wife near the age of her step-children. Her brilliant ability on the piano and her fine contralto voice, plus a loving disposition, no doubt made up for any defects in housekeeping.

Papa Ford died rich in years, wealthy in family, loved by all, remembered in his music, but with nothing in the bank!

# TRADESMEN

Retailing was very much geared to the customer. Money was tight, jobs scarce and few families had motor cars. If shopping required a bus or tram journey this was a very real drain on many budgets. Each community therefore supported the local parade of shops, or walked to the High Street for special purchases.

Shopping in Ilford consisted of two main types: buying all food and most household requirements at the door or, alternatively, from the local 'pantry' shops. A daunting backlog of housework always meant that visiting tradesmen were welcome; on the other hand, if the four walls of the house appeared as a prison for fractious children and distracted mother, then a walk to the shops would be a pleasant release, also acting as a safety valve against frustration. Either way the choice of commodities was comprehensive.

In the mid 20s Sandyhill Road had regular calls from the milkman in his two-wheeled horse-drawn contraption containing churns of milk, a plunger for keeping the cream in circulation and a half pint and one pint metal measure for pouring milk into the customer's jug. If Mother was out she would leave the jug on the doorstep with a saucer as a lid or bead fringed muslin cover as a protection against flies. Every front garden, however small, had a gate and fence; dogs were unable to sniff or foul. Houses with only pavement frontage displayed jugs on window sills. We were fascinated by the slick pouring of milk and the extra half ladleful added for good measure, and no doubt as goodwill gestures against fierce competition. Many housewives offered apple cores or sugar lumps to the horse which at regular stops

*Three generations of milk delivery vehicles*
*(Photographed at the Museum of East Anglian Life, Stowmarket)*

refused to budge unless this happened. At the end of the road a nosebag of sweet smelling chaff and oats was fixed over his muzzle for elevenses and, as he tossed the bag in the air to catch the dregs, pigeons and sparrows arrived to clear spilt seed.

Very soon, wide necked bottles appeared with waxed cardboard discs forced into the lip recess to retain the milk. At first, in prising these out, it was possible to eject milk a few yards across the room, as the disc collapsed into the milk under thumb pressure. Soon, however, enterprise improved the design with a partially cut circle in the middle, which could be prised up with a knife and then pulled out. Competition soon produced another improvement using red tabs attached to one side for lifting the disc without effort or spillage. The final refinement before aluminium caps appeared in the late 30s was 'slogan' discs, printed with advertisements for eggs or butter.

Before enhanced keeping qualities through pasteurisation became the norm, milk was delivered daily, including Christmas and Boxing Days.

Even though Ilford was densely built up there was one milkman who still had a field of cows and a ramshackle cowshed with a primitive dairy attached in which raw unpasteurised milk was bottled for local delivery. His muscular and handsome young delivery man wore white shirts open to hairy lower chest in both summer and severest winter and captivated children by tossing full bottles to shoulder height to catch at waist level as he whistled his way up front paths. Women often kept him talking at the front door, and we heard incomprehensible rumours that Mrs You-Know-Who often paid her bill the old fashioned way. Even our mother patted her hair before opening the door to him. He fell from grace when we persuaded him to throw the same bottle again; he obliged, but unfortunately the milk bottle disc could not stand the extra strain and the contents splashed over the tiled path as the slippery bottle slid from his grasp to crash over our doorstep. His consternation reduced his 'macho' image in our eyes and Mother ceased to pat her hair when he called each day.

Small country towns and larger villages had milk delivered from three wheeled carts; the front single wheel was swivelled for steering and behind the two rear wheels were handles for pushing. On board was a large lidded churn and on the sides hung pint and half pint measures.

On rare visits to Hainault or Abridge we saw butchers' carts similar in design to horse-drawn milk drays, but including rectangular wooden compartments perforated with holes to ventilate the meat within; also providing easy access for flies! In Ilford, with its many butchers' shops, the local itinerant butcher had long since gone: probably just as well from a health point of view as flies were kept at bay in shops with fans and sticky fly-papers until refrigerated counters appeared many years later.

I cannot remember fish ever being hawked from cart or van, but once a week we ate cod (boiled and smothered in parsley sauce) bought from the local fishmongers at Ilford Broadway, reckoned to be a cut above the other smaller shops in Ilford Lane because large blocks of ice were unloaded daily from a horse-drawn cart on to a trolley for trundling around the back where it was hacked into pieces, lasting for most of the morning on the slabs. Nobody could explain to Twin and me why the ice blocks were sea green. We invented adventure stories of brave ice-men chopping ice floes at the North Pole for transport to Ilford fish shops. The ice-man, draped in sacking and wielding large pincers for handling heavy blocks of ice, was, in our eyes, a very mysterious and romantic figure.

20

On windy days dust and dried horse manure whirled on to the ice and fishmongers' slabs. In residential streets the frequent offerings from delivery horses were quickly and eagerly scooped into buckets for personal garden use or, if by resourceful children, sold for a penny a bucket to anybody willing to support such infant enterprise. High Streets were different: it was too dangerous to risk the traffic and trams and therefore droppings were left to dry and be disintegrated by wheels. I suffered from conjunctivitis on several occasions as a result; the family doctor eventually prescribed plain lens glasses as a protection, but Father rebelled against one so young having to be saddled with such an impediment and advised me to keep my eyes shut when the wind gusted: this worked.

Without refrigerators, every wise family cooked bought fish immediately on arrival home, even so, I recall cod with a strong ammonia taste and phosphorescent appearance after cooking. Fishmongers wore straw boaters and full length aprons and looked healthy, invariably with red shiny faces. It seemed to us butchers were similar, but redder and fatter.

After the long walk from Ilford Broadway Mother sometimes rinsed fish in salt water before cooking. Smoked or salted fish was a different matter, keeping fresh longer; when cooked in the evening for Father's late supper, we were sometimes allowed downstairs for a small piece on bread and butter, as an extra-special treat. It was probably only about 8 o'clock, but seemed much later and therefore was a special indulgence. In the winter Father often came home with bloaters or fresh herrings to broil over the dining room fire on a wire grid. One advantage of open fires was that the smell of burning fat had a chimney escape.

Bread was delivered in a two wheeled two legged and roofed trolley with hand shafts between which the delivery man walked to lift and pull rather like a rickshaw man. We were allowed to help, which normally meant scooping up handfuls of fragrant crumbs. Being near the beginning of his round, the bread was still warm and smelt delicious. To save unnecessary walking he would fill a flat wicker basket with a selection of loaves, rolls, buns and cakes in the hope that this would suffice. Mother entertained a great deal and often needed more than that offered from his basket. We were flattered at being allowed to run to the trolley to select extra loaves. With a pencil stub from behind his ear, each sale was recorded in a red Woolworth's notebook for Saturday 'pay up' day. How the economics of this excellent service worked I have no idea; bread was the cheapest of all food and must have been a low profit commodity, yet the daily delivery man was neat, clean, well dressed and spoken, and living in a worthy terraced cottage in Chadwell Heath. His wages were, apparently, adequate and he was devoid of that sadly all-too-common hang-dog expression of so many travelling salesmen of his time.

Near Ilford Broadway on Saturdays an old woman presided over a brazier cooking beetroot, which she hauled out of the water in a wire basket to sell whilst still steaming. Near her another old woman offered celery from an enormous wicker basket; locally grown and unwashed, she said, but from the blackness of the earth around the stems, it probably came from the Fens.

Greengrocery was delivered to the front door from a three wheeled James bike; the front wheel and the handlebars were pure motorbike, plus windshield, saddle and footrests: behind the driver was mounted a two wheeled van body. The shallow wicker basket used for tempting the housewife at the door was a marketing work of art. Several fruits and vegetables were artistically arranged on rhubarb

22

or cabbage leaves, both to entice and, hopefully, remind the buyer of her requirements. Mother was so taken with the artistry one day she asked the salesman whether he did it himself. "No, ma'am," he replied, "my missus does it for me." Mother was not very artistic herself, but appreciated the gift in others. "Clever woman," she said, "does it help your sales?" He grinned politely and shook the hide pouch slung from one shoulder in which he carried the clinking takings.

Quality had to be good with money so scarce, and great care was taken by housewives to check that delivered produce came up to the standards of sample displays. Twin and I were always disappointed that Mother's order, when brought to the door in her own basket, never looked as tempting as the greengrocer's. We also thought him clever to remember orders without writing them down; possibly why there was no response to our chatter as we watched him executing Mother's order from the back of his van.

A favourite travelling salesman was the Carwadine man, with horse-drawn cart crammed with paraffin, polish, pots, mops, pans, brushes, soap, dusters, pails and Zebo grate polish. Articles hung from hooks, some were wedged in racks and every nook and cranny had an article neatly stowed. Mother was sure the salesman was an ex-sailor and had learnt neatness at sea, as had her grandfather. We liked him, as he encouraged us to give the horse sugar lumps and only attempted to order us about on one occasion, when we were standing underneath the vast belly unaware of imminent hazards soon to splash in the gutter.

Many tradesmen used mules to pull their carts. We thought them distinguished with their long ears and reputation for vicious kicking and occasional obstinacy.

The local grocer, Mr Goodall, a fat, comfortable man, attended twice a week on his bicycle to receive Mother's grocery order. Whenever there was a pause in her ordering he would recite in a patient chant "Cocoa, tea, biscuits, custard powder, mustard, eggs..." until an item jogged her memory. That same day his young son would arrive on a delivery bicycle with a huge metal carrier over the front wheel crammed with Mother's order. A grubby invoice with rubber stamped address was handed over and checked and ticked against each item before the boy was allowed to go. "I'll be in on Friday," Mother would say as he closed the gate.

We always accompanied her to pay the bill in anticipation of being offered soft broken biscuits to munch on the way home. Although a small shop it held a vast range of produce. Sacks of white and brown sugar leant against the mahogany counter with nickel plated scoops lying in the mouths; when weighed it was poured neatly into thick blue paper bags, as were prunes, currants, sultanas, mixed dried fruit and butter beans. Nothing was pre-packed. Tea from tall canisters covered with pictures of the East could be bought in ounces to be packed in white paper packets. Golden syrup could be bought in pennyworths if you took your own jar to be filled from the cask. Mother used a lot of treacle and always bought the tins. All eggs were free range, although that term had not been invented, and were generally about a shilling [5p] a dozen. Scarce in winter, most housewives bought dozens in late autumn to pickle in isinglass for winter use in cooking where the musty taste was camouflaged.

Smoked bacon joints behind a glass screen waited selection for slicing into rashers on the hand--operated machine. Mother was asked whether she wanted thick, thin or medium; she always had thin. Cooked slowly in a lidded frying pan, shrivel was

*Delivery bicycle, as used by grocers and butchers*
*(Photograph by courtesy of Mr Jack Wilby)*
*Author and Sam, the paraffin man, with his Model T Ford still*
*in use in Caithness, 1937*

minimal. Butter, salted or fresh, was hacked from lumps and shaped into rectangular pieces using wooden butter pats, dipped in water as a lubricant. Greaseproof paper on large rollers was torn off in required sizes and slickly and neatly used to make a packet very nearly as immaculate as present-day machine-wrapped butter.

If any order placed in the shop was large and heavy for Mother to carry Mr Goodall would arrange for his boy to deliver later that day. If she was entertaining and needed cooked ham, the joint would be selected after careful and often anxious discussion, and the grocer's wife, also large and comfortable, would cook it the day before needed, and junior delivered it exactly on time. The delicious smell of cooked smoked ham as the greaseproof was peeled off, remains with me still. We were both allowed to join Mother in eating the outside slices in our fingers to make sure the Goodalls had done the job properly. Sometimes they had done the cooking so well that we were allowed to join Mother in another slice eaten in our fingers: doubly nice to be breaking the rules of table manners.

Tricycles with box containers in front of the saddle and a driving wheel at the back were popular on the level roads of Ilford. The cat-meat man used one, calling every week with cooked, sliced horse meat on wooden skewers for one old penny. They smelt appetising, but Twin and I, having nibbled a sample, were not surprised our pampered cat preferred cooked fish heads.

Ice cream salesmen from Walls and Eldorado tricycled slowly from road to road like bell-ringing sour-faced Pied Pipers until children appeared clutching pennies. We wondered why ice cream men were always tired and irritable, but Mother said it wasn't surprising as, poor men, and how awful, they only had work for about ten weeks every year.

The muffin man steered his tricycle with one hand clanging a brass handbell with the other, whilst shouting unintelligible sentences ending in "...FINNS." He enjoyed a roaring trade in winter when every house had at least one fire of glowing coals. We were allowed to toast our own before the dining room fire on three pronged brass toasting forks, but Mother insisted on buttering them herself, as we used too much. Margarine bore no resemblance to today's product, it was only used for cooking in certain heavily flavoured puddings or cakes able to smother the awful taste; only the very poor used it on bread - or so we gathered. Our second choice for spreading on bread was beef dripping with pepper and salt. Meat seemed to have more fat between the wars and the dripping (without benefit of refrigeration) was granular and easy to spread, the lucky one had a bonus of brown jelly at the bottom of the dripping basin. Our larder was an unventilated cupboard in the hall: frequently the dripping grew mould which was removed before we helped ourselves.

Home made jam often tasted alcoholic and the cheese, kept in a china dish with lid, was normally sweaty. Bowel problems were called 'summer diarrhoea' and never linked with unhygienic storage. Victorian houses had 'keeping' cellars equipped with cool slate slabs, but many post Great War houses were without anything at all. Householders rigged up wiremesh boxes on shady walls as meat safes.

Twin and I have stood in open mouthed amazement as Father tapped a joint of cooked meat to remove maggots into the sink. Reading the disgust on our faces he said, "Once upon a time they used to use maggots to clean wounds."

# MORE COMMERCE

During the distressing and severe post-war slump in the 1920s parents offered sons and daughters for employment from door to door.

A large, voluminously-clad woman in dusty black stood on our doorstep with a pudgy faced girl lurking shyly behind her. "Good morning, Lady, would you be needin' a hard worker in the house. My girl here is strong, healthy and reliable and only needs a chance. She can wash, clean and iron..." Her voice tailed off as she read the expression on Mother's face and, although not actually told we could not afford extra help, she had that sixth sense born of experience hearing many housewives making excuses in hundreds of identical houses in scores of monotonous streets in those grim slump days.

Mother was genuinely sorry not being able to employ such girls and also agonised, as any mother would, over somebody having to 'sink so low' as to offer a daughter for housework. We sensed this sadness as we all watched mother and daughter trek dejectedly up the garden path next door to discover our neighbour was out, as were many others in our row - some genuinely, others pretending.

Tired men in neat, clean, but worn clothing would also come with boys of 14 years old, fresh from Council School, offering their sons for work in the garden. "He's a willing lad, missus, he'll do anything, honest as the day's long... weedin', mowin', tidyin'... whatever you want, lady." Mother looked at the pathetically thin boys in short grey cut down from father's trousers, with neatly darned jerseys and indeterminately badged school caps and always said, "We're alright, thank you, but would he like a piece of my gingerbread?" Mother's gingerbread was gooey, black and heavenly!

Although we could not explain in words we knew why she cuddled us after the front door was shut on those sad scenes and why she always said, "How lucky **we** are." During lunch on such days Mother was silent and staring out of the French doors as we munched our way through wholesome food. We soon learned not to leave any fat, potatoes, outside crusts of steak and kidney pie or thick white stodge of steak and kidney pudding. "That poor, thin little boy you saw the other day could really do with what you've left... **Eat it up!**"

Two other sad episodes burnt their way into our memories from those hard days. One day the door bell rang and, as was our custom, Twin and I opened the door. Leaning on the brickwork was a thin-faced, pallid man with an anxious, droopy woman clutching a basket. "Hello, sonny, is Mummy in?" he asked. We soon found her and, from behind her skirts, listened to the conversation.

The woman came forward, saying, "Good morning, ma'am... my husband is just recovering from the consumption and they've sent him home. His job's gone, but we've invested in one of them circular knitting machines for making socks. As you have some kiddies, would you be interested in ordering some?"

Mother rather hesitantly talked about my requirements which seemed to be of a rugged nature. An order was given for six pairs of knee length socks with fold-over tops (popular and, in fact, mandatory in schools). "Poor man," said Mother, as they walked slowly towards the gate.

Three weeks later his wife delivered my socks; her husband, she said, was not quite up to making the delivery himself. Mother paid the modest bill and I wore each pair into holes at heel and toe in two or three days! The tension on that primitive

29

home-production-machine through inexperience had been set too low, thus producing a loose knit: Mother had wasted her money. Nevertheless, a week or two later, after not seeming quite as worked up as we would have expected her to be about a bad buy, she walked us along the road leading to Green Lane, where apparently the sock family lived, and furtively pushed an envelope through their door. A few months later, when ominously the curtains were drawn, she went once more with an envelope of coins she had collected in a jam jar on the kitchen window ledge and pushed this through the letter box.

Later on Twin and I heard through the infant grapevine that the family at Number 49 had *lost their dad.* The widow did not appear on our doorstep again and soon there was a change of curtains at 49. Whenever we passed the house on our way to the shops, Mother would sigh by the gate and say, "I wonder what happened to them all?"

Another day we opened the door to a young man wearing thick pebble glasses. His battered tricycle with box container was parked at the kerb. He carried a basket of rubber heels, shoe polish and roughly shaped leather soles. Most people walked a great deal and welded sole shoes with six month guarantees were unheard of; even Uskide rubber soles were stitched to uppers and therefore liable to separate in excessively hard winters, consequently shoes were constantly in need of repair.

Mother was impressed with the enterprise of this polite young man, especially as he explained he was a Dr Barnardo's boy who had learnt cobbling and now started out on his own. She produced a pair of my battered shoes needing leather soling and heeling. After myopic inspection he scribbled on the sole with a pencil stub from behind his ear and quoted what Mother obviously thought a modest

30

price. "Thank you, madam," he said gratefully, "See you next Wednesday."

We asked Mother why he held the shoes so close to his face as if sniffing them, why he wrote on the soles at chin level and why his lips were violet after licking the pencil. "Poor lad," she explained, "he's terribly short-sighted, I only hope he can read what he wrote with that indelible pencil." She told us never to lick such pencils and that we would never be allowed them as they could not be rubbed out.

When the shoes were returned with lop-sided soles, uneven heels and deep cuts in the arches, Mother paid the bill without murmur, but the shoes were ruined and the soles came adrift in a few weeks. Next time he called he was told kindly, "We're alright at the moment, thank you."

There was a feeling in the air that he had heard the same, or worse, elsewhere. He called a few more times, but with the same result; each time Mother was sad and said that it was such a shame but, poor lad, he shouldn't be doing that job. Twin and I liked him and his honest smell of leather and rubber, as we absorbed the tragedy of failure through Mother's emanations of compassion. We were also fascinated by and wanted to try on those thick spectacles.

The old-clothes lady was our most interesting front door experience, not least because of her pungent, unwashed-clothes smell; once smelt a never forgotten mark of 1920s poverty. Her large black clad figure dominated the porch and several layers of skirt prevented us, at our lower level, from all but a glimpse of her diminutive husband hunched forlornly on the donkey cart at the gate.

"Any old clothes, lady. Undies, woollies, sheets, curtains? I give a fair price, lady." Responding to the persuasive intonation Mother produced a canvas bag from the hall cupboard, full of discarded clothes past redemption. These were unceremoniously tipped out to be tied together using sleeves or belts for hooking into a hand-held spring balance; after considerable silent deliberation from the woman and anxiety from Mother, the weight was announced quickly as clothes were unhitched and sixpence or less was offered. Sometimes Mother protested, but the answer was always that she could try better elsewhere. Reluctantly a deal was invariably clinched at the last minute as black skirts began to swirl gate-wards. Money from a deep apron pocket changed hands before the vendor changed her mind; husband alert to the sound of coins began to activate the donkey.

We gathered from her thoughtful silence that Mother felt she had 'been done'. After closing the front door she marched through the house, opening windows to clear the awful smell.

Twin and I felt sad whenever our old and loved clothes were roughly spread over the front doorstep to be carried away in a smelly sack. There was comfort in the smell of our well-worn clothes not found in tickly new garments smelling of shops.

In the suburban culture of the times it was not the done thing to admit to selling old clothes at the door, but most hard pressed housewives did, and were glad of the few extra pence. Some of the kitchen shelf jam jar money for that unfortunate sock maker came from deals with the old clothes buyer. By the time we reached kindergarten school age the old woman had disappeared; the last we saw of her was in Ilford Lane, still in voluminous black and standing in the gutter. "Don't stare," said Mother, "Poor dear, she has a weakness. Oh, how awful. Come along."

Nobody else ever called for old clothes. Rag and bone men patrolled the road from time to time shouting, "Any ole rags?", but it was up to the housewife to wave them down.

Most houses were heated by coal fires (generally only the one, except on Sundays) and often coal delivery carts were in our road with their smell savoured; steaming horse and damp coal was a wonderful combination and in humid weather could be detected by keen young noses even before the cart came round the corner. Unlike most tradesmen, coalmen seemed to us surly and rather frightening, with blackened faces and gruff voices. Mother frequently had altercations with them. She would order ten bags, then open the side gate and, from behind the kitchen curtain, count the number delivered; when the door knocker signified completion, Mother would say, "I only heard **nine** bags!" The coalman bristled, "Alright, lady, count the empty bags yourself." He then lifted each empty bag from the pile by the back door, counting slowly as each was dropped with aggressive, almost insolent, plonks. Inevitably, there were always ten bags. Mother was never convinced of his honesty and, when we said one day, "Mum, why does the coalman always put an empty bag by the coalhole before he brings the **first** full bag?", she knew her instincts were right!

Charringtons delivered after that, with Mother watching that no empty bag was delivered first. Whether or not an empty bag was added to the pile at the end of the delivery will never be known. At any rate, she seemed to be free from the worry of 'being done' from then on.

In dry weather the coal and the coke were normally wet on delivery; we puzzled over this. When Father installed a coke burning Ideal boiler he needed to make a drainage channel from the coke bunker. One day we heard his protestations about wet fuel; he was told that coke had to be hosed down in dry weather to avoid dust nuisance to customers. Sometimes we watched this hosing in the coke yards

33

near the railway and longed to be allowed to hold a hose to make black pools in our own garden. The significance of wetting before weighing for the so-called benefit of the customer was lost on us. I'm sure it was not lost on Father who, many years later, when we were in business together, used to say, when we were confronted with petty pilfering or clandestine employee manufacturing enterprises using our materials and machines in our time, "Don't muzzle the ox that treads the corn". Maybe one reason why our employees were loyal to the firm and would work extra hard, without exhortation from the works' manager, whenever we faced serious competition, and why they sent representatives to his funeral 24 years after he retired.

A persistent and eventually successful doorstep salesman was the vacuum cleaner man. Neat and dapper, in double fronted navy blue suit and rather too black pencil line moustache, he managed to enter our hall one day without appearing to push. From a side pocket, to our open mouthed astonishment, he produced and scattered damp sawdust on our carefully brushed hall carpet (carpets were rarely fitted, but more likely to be strips, with lino or stained boards surrounding). A mark of the good housewife was the regular lifting of edges to sweep out dust and grit with dustpan and brush; slovens, of course, swept dirt under the carpet, thus dispensing with dustpans.

Mother began to bristle as the vacuum cleaner salesman stepped back to view his mess. "Have you a plug nearby, madam?" (In order to make it sound genteel, he made it sound like 'modom').

"Er, er, in the drawing room," said Mother using her choked, holding-back-irritation voice we knew could mean trouble.

"Watch this miracle of science. The kiddies will also enjoy this," said the unwelcome visitor, plugging in his machine. Admittedly the damp sawdust disappeared as the droning noises increased, but Mother was still offended by his pushiness and unspoken suggestion that **her** house needed vacuuming, so she said she would consider the machine when her hand--operated Ewbank carpet sweeper was worn out. We knew she was impressed, as the gleam of desire in her eyes reminded us of how she looked when poring over the Ideal boiler brochures.

As if to cover up her interest and assert her authority at the same time as putting him in his place, she said brusquely, "Hurry up and clear the hall, my husband is coming home early."

That night, as usual, Father was late home, but the slam of the front door woke us. As always, we strained our ears for snippets of adult conversation (one advantage of bungalow living). Wafting under the door on the aroma of macaroni cheese was Mother's voice, enthusiastically describing the vacuum cleaner and how (to our surprise) she knew instinctively and at once that the salesman was honest and reliable. A low, mumbling, but sympathetic response from Father and then Mother saying, "Well, it **would** be a help, especially with the Twins." At this mention we felt important as we sank back into sleep.

Shortly afterwards, the smart little man arrived with a new machine and, for good measure, vacuumed our immaculate (as we thought) front room carpet and, with the attachments, the three piece suite. He emptied a very full dustbag on to newspaper for Mother to save and shew 'Hubby' how wise he was to authorise the acquisition.

Our parents always paid cash or waited until the money was saved before making any purchase, but the 'never-never' or 'glad-and-sorry' was becoming popular between the wars, both in village and suburb. A tally-man on bicycle, cart or, later, in a van called with goods, generally footwear and clothing in many sizes, which could be left with the purchaser after a first payment of a few pence. He would then call regularly, often every week, to collect the following payments. Transactions were negotiated by the tally-man with the customer without reference to a head office. This required considerable understanding of human nature, to say nothing of perseverance, travelling in all weathers. At a discreet moment, shrewdly chosen by the experienced tally-man, he would offer other items he discerned were needed, assuring himself of a continuing reason for calling and collecting small weekly sums.

The system worked efficiently and, although only impartial observers, we had a close friend in the business who informed us of all the wrinkles, successes and failures, and who did so well himself he eventually opened a small clothing shop, which he and his wife ran until they retired to Brentwood, in what was then called 'comfortable circumstances'.

Other regular callers at the house included dustmen; an event of great interest every week. We waited with enthusiasm for these large, hob-nail booted men to clump their way up the path to grab the (unlined) dustbin and swing in one smooth movement on to their leather padded shoulders. The weight was considerable because of the ashes and clinker. Balancing the heavy bin on the rim of the cart it was tipped over in a fog of smelly dust; if bins contained soggy messes stuck to the bottom it was because nobody wrapped rubbish. Then the bin was slammed on the cart's reinforced edge until the muck was dislodged: dustbins soon became battered and bent until the metal lid no longer fitted properly. The men's faces were ash covered, with only eyes and lips clearly discernable. We admired

36

the way they swirled powdered Jeyes fluid disinfectant in one slick movement to coat the empty bin. Unlike today, the lidded bin was replaced in its habitual place and the side gate carefully closed. Every Christmas the foreman knocked to wish us a Happy Christmas and Mother gladly gave him two shillings, which was generous in those days.

We loved the enormous and benign draught horse and were allowed to stroke his neck before offering sugar lumps, which he delicately removed from our palms. Afterwards we were ordered to wash our hands and faces free from dust and Jeyes powder before being allowed at table. As animal lovers, Twin and I discussed how nice it was to see the foreman loved his horse and spoke to him as a friend. "C'm'on, Boyee," he would say in gruff tones and the horse would immediately move a few houses along; never did he need to be told to stop.

A friend took us to the stables one day and we recognised 'our' horse, but were disappointed when he seemed to prefer the hay trough.

One of the most regular callers at our door was a soberly clad woman known as the Step Lady, who would scrub the stone step in front of the house for sixpence [$2\frac{1}{2}$p]. Ilford had thousands of stone steps and many housewives who did not wish to be seen scrubbing. Twin and I, receiving one old penny per week as pocket money, thought she was grossly overpaid and we offered to scrub our modest slab, but Mother was reluctant; we had a hunch she feared the neighbours would think she was exploiting her children and, in any case, it was not everybody who could afford the Step Lady!

# SHOPPING

Most shopping trips involved a call at the below-
pavement lavatories near Ilford Market. Small boys
always shared ladies' facilities with mothers, sisters
or aunts. It was a friendly arrangement; visitors
were met with a cheery "Mornin', duckie," as the
penny clanged into the brass container/lock. When
the door swung open the janitor advanced from her
cubby hole, flourishing a towel, and sailed into the
paid-for cubicle, wiping the seat with a flourish,
"There y'are, dearie" was added for goodwill as she
bustled out, leaving behind a smell of mothballs and
milk stout. When leaving, Mother always said,
"Thank you. Good morning," and the dignified slow
nod of head in response implied acknowledgement
of personal service being appreciated by a discerning
client!

Apart from park and public house open air
lavatories, all public conveniences seemed to have
attendants; extremely good value for one real penny
for females, generally free for males, and also a
safeguard against vandalism and importuning. Those
rarer lavatories in unsavoury areas and simply
designated WOMEN were generally unfit to sit upon
and unroofed urinals at the rear of public houses
or near tram depots, or whatever, marked MEN had
nowhere to sit.

Opposite the lavatories was Ilford Market, a
covered draughty place with booming echoes. Early
in the morning wet tea leaves were strewn at right
angles across the walkways to absorb dust, as they
were swept into piled by shag smoking men wielding
wide brooms, often leaving strips of unswept pavement because of poor light, poor pay or poor
motivation. Occasionally supplies of damp tea

leaves became scarce; sticky sawdust, smelling of oil and shaken out of leaking sacks, was used instead. I believe this was called 'Dusmo', a brilliant designation for a good practical product.

Mother, like us, found Ilford Market fascinating. However, she rarely bought anything. Traders, quick witted East Londoners, were rather too forceful for somebody guarding such a slender purse as she carried in those days. The brilliantly lit dress shops, with names like Rosenbaum's Gowns, drew her as a magnet and, holding one of us in each hand, she worked her way along the windows. We were more interested in the sharp-eyed salespeople, discreetly and shrewdly watching every move she made. When Mother lingered near a particularly desirable frock a smartly dressed man with unctuous manner emerged, "That would suit you, madam, **just** your colour." We felt the tensing hand as she said, "I'm only looking." Invariably at this point a woman with jet black or auburn hair (both too intense in colour to be real, Mother said) appeared quietly and, with carefully smoothed voice, invited Mother to bring the kiddies in and try on a dress or two in comfort in front of a full length mirror.

Only once did she succumb. Twin and I went behind the curtain with her as she removed her dress. The recommended latest model was handed in and, as soon as the swish of the descending dress over artificial silk was heard, the lurking assistant peered through the curtains.

"Absolutely YOU, madam," said she, smoothing the folds and creases. "Come out and look in the full length mirror." She made this sound like a special privilege. Holding spare material firmly in the small of the back she steered Mother to the mirror. From the front the dress looked reasonable.

Painstakingly hoarded housekeeping money was soon handed over. Mother's pace increased as we neared Sandyhill Road. Tea was late because of the stumping about upstairs and, when at last she came down, we detected from her expression it would be wise to be quiet and well behaved at tea and when being prepared for bed. Whenever there were doubts about a purchase she was always irritable and un-reasonable. Fortunately, Father who always knew how to handle such moods, came home early that night and, as we dipped fingers of bread and butter in his boiled egg we heard him say, "No, no, no, the material is exactly right for you. We'll get Miss Tarpin to make it fit. I'll pay for it. Now, let's put the Twins to bed."

Miss Tarpin was a peripatetic dressmaker only contactable by letter as her thickly net-curtained house always appeared to be empty. Her system was to eat and work in the customer's house using what-ever sewing machine was available. She could alter or make anything, ranging from underwear to dresses, coats, suits (male or female), soft furnishings and curtains. Full board, apart from bed, was required and the fee for work to be negotiated and agreed in genteel manner beforehand. Whatever it was must have been modest as it came out of Mother's £1/10/- housekeeping money.

We found Miss Tarpin absolutely engrossing with a black velvet ribbon holding the folds in her neck together, a cold nose acting as a permanent water condenser, thus requiring refined sniffing at frequent intervals, and oval, steel framed spectacles, half-way down her nose, resting securely in a reddened indentation at exactly the right place.

If Mother suddenly required a change in hem line or style not the subject of preliminary negoti-ation, sniffing became more pronounced with throat clearing added, before saying, in a slightly louder and firmer tone, "**That** would take a **lot** longer..." [strategic pause]"... but of course, if you...?" Mother

40

recognised the hint of expensive fee re-negotiation and generally abandoned the new idea.

Auntie Tarpin, as we resented having to call her, normally exuded the smell of lavender water, but her breath often smelt of biscuits, not surprising as she frequently dipped into the biscuit barrel when having her mid-morning cup of tea, in the same vague, absent minded manner in which she ate lunch. Twin and I noticed that sometimes she smelt of the fluid Father used for cleaning his typewriter, in which case she went to the biscuit barrel more often.

Mother, generous in many ways, became mean with biscuits and soon Miss Tarpin was rationed to two in her saucer. The biscuit barrel was confined to the sideboard cupboard between refreshment times, instead of pride of place on top. Her appetite for such a thin person seemed, to us, immense. Sometimes we felt deprived as she received huge helpings of steak and kidney pudding, leaving only a small amount for second helpings. Much to our annoyance, one day she accepted the last portion of boiled beef and carrots: Twin burst into tears, eventually confessing between sobs that she wanted more. Miss Tarpin, after a massive sniff, carefully forked off a portion from her plate on to Twin's. Louder sobs ensued, as we were both very fussy about other people's dirty plates, cups and utensils. As children everywhere, we were expert at visually dividing food fairly on dishing-up plates. Subsequent rectification of inequalities never quite overcame the initial resentment.

When new lounge curtains were required from Miss Tarpin on a certain date, rapidly approaching, her helpings of foods were, so it seemed to us, gauged according to urgency. "Can you do them in time?" said Mother anxiously. "Oh, I'm sure I can, providing this cotton holds out!" Miss Tarpin always hedged her bets.

Then followed discussions about providing suitable extra cotton for finishing the order. Wisely she never produced her own supplies of thread, cloth, needles, thimbles or patterns. If things went wrong it was always the fault of the customers' materials or unreasonable demands.

Twin and I, in addition to resenting the universal custom of addressing female family friends as 'aunty' also took umbrage at her intimate habit of removing broad bean skins in her mouth to offer us the soft green insides as titbits from her fork.

Hand-me-downs, passed-ons and grown-out-ofs were part and parcel of living in the twenties, and the Miss Tarpins of that world performed a useful service adapting clothing to the latest needs or in producing something new from material bought, swapped, inherited or used again after laborious unpicking. My first cricket trousers were Tarpin-made from an old sheet. I was mortified, because a well-off cousin told me **proper** cricket trousers were flannels and made from wool/cotton mixtures or wool and therefore had a cream tinge. Mine being cotton and dutifully and lovingly washed were snow white, but easily creased and of obvious origin. My chagrin was partly due to loyalty to Mother, who had done her best on limited resources and was devoid of any cricket experience in her tennis playing family of five girls and one horse-mad boy.

Midweek shopping often involved visits to the larger Ilford stores, such as Bodgers or Wests. The swing or revolving doors were the first thrills, soon tempered by the sobering effect of bodeful shop-walkers generally dressed in black single-breasted jackets and striped trousers or, more rarely, well groomed women in dark dresses and with severe expressions under well-coiffured hair.

Requirements were politely requested and then instructions given, "First floor, madam, second counter on the right." Sometimes Mother only intended to buy one reel of cotton while having a good look round, but she would say, "Haberdashery, please." and take her time getting there.

The highlight was the ingenious system of paying for even the smallest purchases. Every counter had two overhead wires leading directly to a central raised glass-sided cubicle in which presided a stern-faced efficient woman cashier. Counter staff unhitched a small cylindrical container hanging from the overhead wires, removed the lid, placed the invoice and money inside, replaced the container on to the return wire and then, with a movement that fascinated us, pulled a lever which catapulted invoice and money along the wire (like a ski-lift gone mad) to clang into the central counting-house for the cashier to unload, check, provide change, enclose rubber stamped receipt, and hurtle it back to the counter. The sales lady would cease her small talk, hand over the reel of cotton Mother had chosen and slickly unscrew the container holding change and receipt; after carefully checking she would pass receipt and money to Mother and bid us "Good day". All this for just a few pence.

On busy days we would walk through the store with constant whirring noises from aerial money and the clang of returning receipts, instead of the till bells of the smaller establishments. Clutching the printed paper bag containing an insignificant purchase and trying to make it look more important, we approached the exit. The sharp-eyed, but discreet, shopwalker would open the doors, while saying, "Thank you, madam".

When, rarely, Mother bought sheets or anything more substantial, we imagined the shop-walker had a warmer tone and was more deferential as he swept the doors open for us. If, on entering, Mother said, "Curtaining," he would flick his fingers towards the

43

relevant counter, shouting, "Forward please, Miss Clarke." Mother straightened her back and even we felt important. It was a clever system which, in a subtle way, gave customers a feeling of welcome, kept the staff alert and, no doubt, provided an easy, up-to-date way of informing management of trends, requirements or failures: it was possibly also a deterrent to would-be shop-lifters.

Overhead railway accounting procedures, with all conveyance wires radiating from the central cashier to each sales counter was the mark of a **store**, whilst mahogany sliding-drawer tills, with each movement activating a pinging bell, were marks of a **shop**. Slightly more sophisticated shops had reels of paper driven by each outward movement of the till drawer, so that each transaction could be recorded in pencil by the saleslady. Regardless of the time, nobody was allowed home until the manager had checked all till rolls against counter receipts. If the float (the small change placed in the till before opening time) was not exactly right according to the sales recorded, then everybody stayed behind until the problem was solved. A friend of ours told us she slipped a shilling into the till one Saturday night to make up a deficiency to avoid being late for meeting her 'young man' taking her to the Palais de Dance that evening. She added that, because he willingly paid her promised share of the tickets in view of her sacrifice, she was sure he would make a good husband!

Tills were cleverly crafted in mahogany. Drawers, approximately four inches deep, had scooped out indentations for pennies, ha'pennies and farthings near the front, then separate places for half-crowns, florins, shillings, sixpences and silver threepenny bits. Sovereigns had a special slot at the back of the till. Paper money was placed under mousetrap-type clamps; rare five pound notes in

44

white crackly paper had to be passed by the manager and, even then, often signed with name and address by the customer. Unless extremely well known locally it was better to change down for smaller denominations at the bank. Britain abandoned the Gold Standard in the slump of 1931 and the smaller sized sovereign issued from 1817 to 1917 gradually became a collector's piece if it hadn't been cashed.

Twin and I can only dimly remember any relative actually tendering a sovereign for a purchase. Father, however, often told us of the time when, as a seventeen year old working in a Bedford bank before the Great War, he was detailed off one day to deliver 500 golden sovereigns in a canvas bag to another bank in Northampton. He said they were terribly heavy and the bags clearly labelled: nobody seemed to worry about security. His main worry was whether he could spread his few pence allowance for travel and lunch to cover two brown rolls with his two penn'orth of dates or make do with only one.

Dates provide an interesting example of how the value of money has changed in this century. For instance, in 1920 for the equivalent of five new pence it was possible to buy four pounds of loose dates. In 1947 they would most likely be blocked into solid lumps at the equivalent of 15 new pence, admittedly without stones, but at least pasteurised, grit and the odd escapee included. In 1991 the same weight would cost over £5.

Furniture shops were completely different with their hushed and enormous whisper-echoing caverns, smelling of shellac lacquer. Each floor contained dozens of lavishly (so we thought) furnished rooms, each with one wall missing adjacent to the walkway for easy viewing or to enable the bold to sample catches, hinges and springs. Salesmen were discreetly hidden in cubicle offices, so that prospective buyers could view in relaxed fashion. We discovered hidden eyes were upon us when, behind Mother's back, we bounced on an inviting moquette settee, enjoying squeaking springs and smells of new upholstery, only to find the second floor salesman, whose approach had been muffled by deep carpeting, glaring at us as he gave an affected cough. Mother, recognising the artificial nature of such a sound, turned from her day-dream viewing of a glass fronted bureau-desk and advanced menacingly towards our by now stationary forms.

"Was madam looking for something in particular?" He used a voice full of delicate restraint with menace well controlled, but ready to be unleashed.

"My husband is considering a new three-piece for the drawing room," said Mother, gripping our hands with what we thought excessive force.

After a pause, he asked, "And maybe a bureau-desk as well?" At this her grip tightened yet more as we were propelled down the stairway and, when out of sight, were reprimanded for doing what we knew we mustn't on the settee in our tiny front room.

There were other shops in the High Street where it could be dangerous to drool or linger over window displays. One sweet shop with bins of bruised chocolate pieces in the porch had the owner hovering and waiting to bend to the level of small children with suggestions for spending pocket money. Twin and I, clutching a Saturday's penny were suckers for offers of bagging up penn'orths of mixtures. We always thought the offer worthwhile, but Mother advocated the pointed-nose woman's shop on the corner as offering better value. One day, an aunt allowed us to spend our pennies on bags of chocolate pieces; we were bitterly disappointed at the stale taste and gritty texture.

Mother was right, the corner shop chocolate toffee slabs broken into a bag with a small brass hammer were much better value. The thin owner never smiled and wore woollen mittens summer and winter, but her stock carried well-known names and was always fresh. We were also allowed, if we wished, to spend our Saturday penny in four separate farthings. Sweets were not displayed for little fingers to filch all too easily, as they are today. We asked for the tray, which was produced from under the counter, to be proferred at our level, but overseen by eagle eye. Gob stoppers, carefully sucked and removed to check which colour was now shewing at regular intervals, would last for about half a mile of slow walking. When staying at Uncle's farm in Kent, where the shops were even cheaper than in the suburbs, a ha'p'orth of chocolate drops would last across the fields from Cobham parish church to Luddesdowne, if rationed to one at each telephone pole.

Twenty ruddy aniseed balls could be bought for one penny and a large roll of liquorice for a farthing. Sherbet dabs in triangular paper packets with sticky toffee knobs on thin wooden skewers for dipping and licking were one penny. From an article in the *Boy's Own Paper* we had gained the impression that sheiks reclined on Persian carpets in their large tents whilst sipping sherbet. Twin and I took it in turns to be the slave, waving palms over reclining figure as we supped. Behind the rocky on a hot day it could be quite exotic.

Late Saturday afternoons near Ilford Broadway greengrocers and butchers would often shout invitations to strollers to snap up bargain cauliflowers, local celery roots or shoulders of Canterbury lamb and, in the cheaper shops, of Argentine beef. Normally Mother was an excellent cook, who could be relied on to produce succulent tender joints, but this beef was a disaster, long grained and tough with a rank taste, most of it subsequently consigned to a shepherd's pie. Father, always discreet and incapable of cooking anything himself, asked where the beef had been bought. When told by tearful Mother, he responded, "Frozen for many weeks in the South American meat boats. No wonder it's tough - not **your** fault, darling." That was the last special offer she bought, but **salted** Argentine beef, boiled with carrots and dumplings appeared on our table several times each winter.

New Zealand lamp (cleverly called Canterbury) was similarly refrigerated, but both parents always maintained it was more tender and sweeter than English. A generous shoulder could be bought for the equivalent of $12\frac{1}{2}$p and would provide us with a hot roast on Saturday, cold on Sunday with one or two guests sharing, chibbles (as Father called them) with home-made chutney on Monday and then blade-bone and knuckle stew on Tuesday - not our favourite, with its rank taste of stale larder-dried meat inadequately camouflaged with butter beans, onions, carrots, pearl barley, pepper and rosemary. The gravy was semi-translucent pale grey and impervious to improvement with vegetables or herbs. When steam from slow simmering filled the house, Mother stirred in a spoonful of Ventacachellum's curry powder: the disguise was not perfect, but at least palatable.

Mother stewed far more dishes than she casseroled to save on gas. Lentils and split peas frequently stuck to the bottom of the saucepan and burnt into solid splodges; when we grew tall enough we took it in turns to stir. Anything was better than having to eat burnt stew!

Occasionally, larger stores in Ilford would rent sales floor space to firms for promoting products deemed too superior for market demonstrations, where quack remedies and gimmicky gadgets, which never worked when bought, were normally hawked. One day in Bodgers in the High Street, we were captivated by a platinum blonde in white blouse and navy blue skirt, who stood on a raised platform in the middle of the ground floor saleroom with a starched white clothed table covered with bottles of peroxide. She had a loud elocution-trained voice, a few grammatical lapses, but confident, almost daunting manner. Her product, she said, would not only bleach hair, but also kill germs. To prove these claims she parted her brittle hair to show dark new hair emerging. We hoped for a demonstration of hair bleaching, but she moved on to germ killing by adding peroxide to a tumbler of water, then with a dramatic flourish she snipped off a small piece of sponge from a block on the table and, using tweezers, after a breathless pause to increase anticipation of the drama to come, she placed the fragment in the tumbler, giving an impression of being a laboratory assistant on important research.

"Watch, ladies, how powerful our product is!" With tumbler held high, the sponge disintegrated into a milky fluid and, after stirring with a glass rod, slowly cleared. "**That** is how our product deals with household germs."

Mother was not impressed, but many were, including Twin and me. On the way home we were told our family did not believe in changing what God had given us as hair colour, and Jeyes Fluid was cheaper for drains, sinks and lavatories, in any case.

A small haberdashery shop in Ilford Lane was popular with us; full of interest and bursting with stock, presided over by two middle-aged ladies with soft voices and limitless patience. Mother said they were 'war spinsters'. The atmosphere was stuffy, the light dim and a rich smell of new woollen underwear, starched cotton and lavender water wafted

49

outside whenever the door opened. Purchases were often small; buttons could be bought singly and, together with a reel of cotton, taken into the daylight for matching colour on a snippet of dress material. Much advice was offered, discussed and accepted with only a few pence changing hands on conclusion.

The solid mahogany counter was topped with a glass showcase full of packets of needles, thimblés, tape, hairclips and other small articles. Above the counter were brass rods hung with dusters, towels, dish cloths, vests, liberty bodices and, sometimes, vast pink corsets. With overhead displays, meagre light was reduced yet further. Each cubby hole or drawer contained a card cut from delivery cartons and neatly lined in pencil for recording the number of articles in stock; after a transaction the number was reduced. When use of the india rubber had rendered the white face of the cardboard to a blotchy fawn, a new piece was cut.

If the shop was big enough to support even one assistant, the stock sheets recorded the cost price in code, so that only the proprietor knew. The only code we were privileged to know was in Grand father's shop. THUNDERCLAPS, based on twelve pence in the shilling, with T standing for number 1, P for eleven and S for nought: thus an article costing twelve shillings and sixpence was coded TH/E. Occasionally some goods were marked S/S, pronounced ess-suss-ess, which meant that had been written down in value at so many stock-takings that they were not in the books and could be sold at a profit at any price. "I've sold an ess-suss-ess for five shillings," would warrant praise from the owner and, possibly if the article was very ess-suss-ess, a share in the profits.

On one of our haberdashery-cum-draper visits a commercial traveller was taking down an order

54

for sundries and we watched the shopkeeper consult her cards before ordering refills. Each time she recorded the date and quantity in brackets at the end of each line to avoid ordering again if another traveller called with similar merchandise. Poor man, he had to wait patiently while customers were served. Mother, a shopkeeper's daughter, felt sorry for travellers, especially when frequently carrying two heavy suitcases of samples and another under the arm. Rarely did they have the luxury of a motor car. Those selling larger items hired barrows to trundle samples from the railway station to each customer. Once or twice we saw a barrow outside the shop with another traveller waiting his turn out of sight around the corner. There was an unwritten courtesy law, whereby no traveller would enter a shop until the other had left the premises.

We were accustomed to the quiet 'refeened' deference offered by the haberdasher to customers and somewhat puzzled by the contrasting authoritative tone she used for the commercial traveller and also her effortless change of face when turning from him to us.

# ADVERTISING

Mass media advertising is becoming more and more elaborate and so 'clever' that in many cases it is difficult to discern exactly what is being advertised - especially noticeable on television. Instead of a board of directors deciding amongst themselves what they wanted to say to encourage sale and then asking an advertising agent to illustrate their precise wishes in art form for poster, magazine or newspaper, we now have highly professional agencies complete with public relations experts constantly thinking up unusual angles so obscure they sometimes appear to be designed more to impress competitor agencies than the buying public.

Between the wars the direct, simple approach was favoured. Most nationally-known firms tried to keep their name before the country with as few words as possible; particularly when splashed along the sides of trams and buses - 'Mazawattee Tea satisfies your finer taste'... 'Enjoy summer health all year round with Ovaltine'... 'Hovis makes vitality a reality'... (or puns as favoured by Bovril) 'Bovril sandwiches 'meat' the situation'.

Our family was more aware of advertisements than most because Father, as a freelance advertising agent, felt free to criticise, comment, approve or disapprove of any displayed in the sparse supply of magazines and newspapers in our frugal household.

Through the barter system Twin and I managed to maintain a furtive supply of tuppenny bloods doomed to instant confiscation if discovered. The small ads fascinated us. I came across a few 1928 *Magnets* when moving house and memories came flooding back. For many years, I was shorter than Twin and if five shillings [25p] had been available

I would have sent for the course from the Stebbing Institute with their **London** address, rather than use use Melvin C Strong far away in Swansea. It did not occur to us that growth is assured in a growing boy without payment, thanks to Mother Nature. P Ross charged two guineas for his system and sported an importantly brief address - P Ross, Height Specialist, Scarborough.

Twin expressed interest in Stebbings' cure for blushing, but was restrained by lack of funds. Tony, a bosom friend with an occasional slight stammer, was attracted by the stammering advertisement 'particulars free' and we composed a letter. At discovering from the reply (in plain brown envelope) it was only the particulars of the price which was free, vocal indignation cured his stammer.

How the economics of tuppenny bloods worked

is difficult to imagine. The printed page measured 6 by $9\frac{1}{2}$ inches with small newspaper sized type. Twenty five sides were capable of approximately two hundred and thirty inches depth of print; of this some thirty seven inches were devoted to story illustration and only thirty inches to advertisements. Nowadays, to survive, magazines need more space devoted to advertisements than to text.

Twin and I resented the space we considered wasted; far better another dramatic picture of Billy Bunter suffering under the 'Prince of Japers', Harry Wharton, and Co. We were particularly incensed at 'Have you a red nose? Send a stamp to pay postage and you will learn how to rid yourself of such a terrible affliction Free of Charge. Mr A Temple (Specialist) Palace House (2nd Floor) Shaftesbury Ave, London W1.

"After all," said Twin, "everybody has a red nose in cold weather, except Cousin Ernie who Gran says likes too many strawberries."

Children's magazines of the period also illustrate how idioms and slang changes in less than a lifetime. Who would dream of referring to a pen as 'corking'?

The football was a 'footer' and you could be 'biffed' by it! Next week's issue would include other 'grand yarns' or even 'ripping tales' and your chums could enjoy the Editor's page, beginning with

Come into the office, boys! Always glad to hear from you, chums, so drop me a line. Are you pleased with this week's topping coloured pictures? Roll, bowl or pitch your queries in to me, chums? I'm here to be shot at. Your Editor

No doubt the boomerang advertisement was in his mind when he wrote that regular letter.

Advertising standards were not so tightly controlled and some undoubtedly sailed rather close to the wind if taken too literally. Medically flavoured approaches were designed to resemble an avuncular family doctor giving easily understood reasons for certain medications

Wake up your Liver bile and you'll jump out of bed in the morning full of vim and vigour. The liver should pour out two pints of liquid bile into your bowels daily. If this bile is not flowing freely, your food doesn't digest. You get headaches and feel rotten. You get constipated. Your whole system is poisoned and you feel sour, slack, and the world looks black.

Laxatives help a little, but a mere bowel movement doesn't get at the cause. It takes good old Carter's Little Liver Pills to get those two points flowing freely and make you feel Up and Up.

55

Harmless, gentle, yet amazing in making bile flow freely. Ask for Carter's Little Liver Pills. Stubbornly refuse anything else.

That approach today would need an explanation of the functioning of liver, pancreatic duct, bile duct and duodenum and possibly be so boring the

# "It is not original sin, but original dirt we have to fight"

## SAYS JOAN SUTHERLAND

*Joan Sutherland is the famous novelist author of THE GOLDEN ALTAR and other popular books. In private life she is Mrs. Richard Kelly, and mother of four lovely children, Dennis, Michael, Angela and June*

"Children are naturally grubby—until the age of nine or so when they begin to develop civilised tastes. Perhaps boys are the worst offenders, but even dainty little girls show extraordinary inclinations at times to burrow in dirt. The chief problem of the nursery is how to fight dirt successfully.

My prescription for healthy nurseries is as follows. Painted walls which can be washed down . . . not only healthier in themselves but far less confusing to the youthful eye than figured wallpaper. Cork lino on all floors. Glazed chintz which can be rubbed clean like any other shiny surface. And last but not least, plenty of VIM."

In a house where there are children, VIM is a necessity. Their health depends on cleanliness, for dirt and disease are inseparably connected. Keep their nursery spotless with VIM. Use VIM for washing up the vessels used in preparing their food, for keeping baths and basins sweet and fresh. It searches out every hidden speck of grime and makes them scientifically clean and germ-free. VIM sweeps through the house like sunshine, leaving cleanliness, wholesomeness and safety in its track.

## Protect your home with

# VIM

★ V I M cleans woodwork, painted or plain, marble and earthenware. Brightens as well as cleans—brass, bronze, copper, taps, saucepans. Does the longest jobs in a few moments—sinks, gas-stove, bath. Cleans stained or grimy hands.

57

advertisement would fail.

In these glue-sniffing days Dr Mackenzie's Smelling Bottle blurb might be considered in bad taste. In 1929 sniffing was something we were ticked off for, "For goodness sake, haven't you twins got handkerchiefs?"

Today, no organisation would dare refer to a product claiming a Great Cure for Colds, Influenza, Catarrh, Hay Fever. Nor would a shampoo manufacturer refer to a product which not only washed, nourished and burnished hair, but also **waved,** as did Butywave for sixpence a packet, including separate packets of lime juice rinsing crystals and Special Egyptian Henna Burnish.

Father said he had no time of money to provide for vanity products; for Twin and me Friday was carbolic Lifebuoy Soap hair washing in the bath with all the attendant problems of soapy water entering nostrils unless pinched tight.

Mother used Vim for sink and bath, but one day showed their half page advertisement to Father. "What do you think of 'It is not original sin, but original dirt we have to fight'. Isn't it a bit, er, er?" asked Mother, waiting for what she knew was coming. "Hmm, taking the Word of God in vain for material gain," said Father. But we still used Vim.

Some advertisements dealt with slightly vulgar subjects in discreet ways. For example, Zenoids for digestion and 'slight indiscretions at meals' and the need for corrective tablets after meals. Twin and I disgraced ourselves by poring over the illustration discussing who had probably made the indiscretion at table and what type it might have been. The picture delicately avoids any hint of the culprit. Unfortunately, we were unaware Father had entered the room, having overheard suspect giggles. "We don't find that sort of talk amusing, give me the magazine and go to your room until your mother

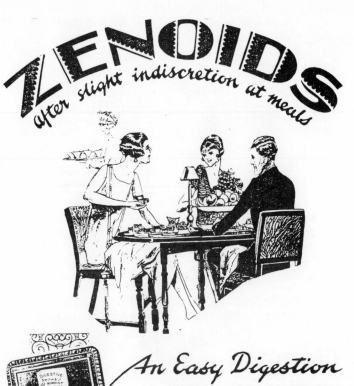

59

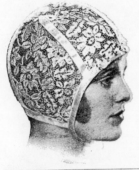
calls you for tea."
Many women in our circle slept with fine mesh
hair nets prolonging the life of their curling-tonged

waves. Some wore even finer mesh for daytime neatness, but nobody we knew ever wore the 'Ladye Jayne' Slumber Helmet. Presumably the unusual spelling was intended to give the product exclusivity and class.

In a 1915 *Cadell's Directory of Gravesend* found amongst my maternal grandmother's effects was a chimney sweep's advertisement. It has an honest, homely air about it, also a delicate tilt at unscrupulous competitors. Clean cloths for upper apartments is a nice touch.

Twice a year in Ilford we slipped a note through the letter box of Mr Larkin, Sweep, asking for his services. In a few days he would call on his way home on ancient motorbike and coffin-shaped lidless sidecar to arrange the great day. Only eyes and mouth were discernible, the rest of him was matt black. His modest logo on the sidecar was indecipherable, because every hessian sack when dumped in the sidecar emitted clouds of soot, which in damp weather settled and stuck. He always came early in the morning, so that our sole heating could be lit in the dining room after breakfast. The whole room was covered with Mother's dust sheets; the floor supplemented with newspaper to save the sheets. He had his own thicker cloth covering the fireplace and the brushes were pushed through a central hole. Rod sections were screwed on and the brush turned regularly as it climbed.

He told us that, when he was learning his trade, he turned the rods the wrong way and the brush unscrewed to remain resting over the chimney pot opening. Mother pressed him to say how it was retrieved. Reluctantly, he admitted he had to climb the roof. "Hope it was a bungalow," said Mother.

His reply was avoided by asking us to run outside and then come a tell him if the brush was visible. After reporting, we rushed out to watch the brush revolve and jerk. As he retracted the rods each was unscrewed, leaving fine soot and brick dust on newspaper in the hearth; disappearing under the cover with a small shovel and sack, he neatly packaged the mess, but although skilful and well practised, the dust sheets were now covered and were set aside for washing. Meanwhile Mother had laid newspaper in the hall and he clumped out, returning later to collect his modest fee, which I think was 'a florin, if you please, ma'am'.

In the lingering smell of soot, Twin and I spent the rest of the morning discussing one of our favourite stories *The Water Babies*, where poor little Tom was forced to climb up inside a vast chimney to dislodge soot for his cruel employer.

One day, when delivering a note to Mr Larkin, his highly polished front door was open and a squeaky clean, kindly Mrs Larkin took the note. Her hall smelt of lavender furniture polish and everything shone; an immaculate black and white cat sat on the bottom stair. Our rude stares at the interior were read by Mrs Larkin, "I can see what you're thinking, dears. I walk him straight through to his shed when he comes home, where he'll find lots of warm water and clean clothes waiting for him."

Vacuum chimney sweeping was a thing of the future, as was the trade description 'Flueologist' I came across recently.

Other excerpts from the 1915 *Directory* of interest include an 8 roomed house with cold greenhouse and long garden offered to rent unfurnished at £24 per annum. Mr A Sleep advertised his skills as 'Bird and Animal Stuffer'. Chas E Dixon, Photographer, was obviously proud he could offer 'Day or Electric Light'. The local laundry 'Work under Perfect Sanitary Arrangements', and a dentist sold false teeth as Artificial Teeth from two shillings and sixpence to ten shillings and sixpence per tooth.

Many advertisers had no telephone numbers, but one tailor printed his as 'One Y One'. What 'Y' stands for is rather baffling, but by the prominence given to telephone numbers of only two digits it was undoubtedly prestigious to own one for the convenience of customers also connected.

Most of us will be familiar with the instruction book translated into English from Japanese. Some literal translations take no account of idioms. In a 1932 *Magnet* there are traces of the same thing in the last sentence of a Jujitsu advertisement.

Don't be bullied.

Send four penny stamps for Two Splendid Lessons in Jujitsu and Handsome Photoplate of Jap Champions. The Wonderful Japanese Self-Defence Without Weapons. Take care of Yourself under All circumstances; fear no man. You can have Monster Illustrated Portion for P.O. 3/9. Send now to Yawara, 10 Queensway, Hanworth, Mddx.

**Laurance D. Ford**
*Individual Attention*
**ADVERTISING**
*93 Levett Gardens*
**SEVEN KINGS**

*Phone. Seven Kings 2167*

*Father's spare time enterprise, 1928/36, drawn for die–stamping by himself*

# CLOTHING

Being dressed for cold weather was an ordeal often leading to tears. In houses devoid of central heating, survival depended on wool. Everybody 'went into wool' from cotton underwear as soon as days shortened. Twin and I dreaded changeover day. Half sleeved round-necked button-fronted all wool vests replaced interlock cotton athletic vests. Wool varied in quality according to price; the cheaper it was the more tickly it became: we suffered in the lower priced bracket. It is true we kept warm, but at vast expense in skin irritation. Coarse wool next to sensitive eczema-prone surfaces can be unbelievably uncomfortable; heat generated by the suffering itself and boosted by energetic scratching only more itching and, in my case, produced weeping blains.

All aunts on Mother's side - Nora, Muriel, Hilda and Kathleen - chided, "If you didn't keep scratching yourself you wouldn't be so sore" and "Big boys don't snivel". Mother followed up ethically, "You are a lucky boy to **have** warm clothing!" Twin wore similar vests, but her skin was wool tolerant. To her credit she never used natural immunity as a means of proving superiority over my tendencies to weep and grumble about clothing. Her vests did, in fact, tickle, but she was blain and complain free.

The next horror to cover vests were woolly combs (short for 'combinations' or, in America 'union suits'). For male adults they had long legs and sleeves, but for us a unisex version (the unisex idea is ancient, even though the term is modern) with short sleeves and legs. Being a one-piece garment with no waist separation, slits back and front were provided lower down for essential purposes; with care, working quite well until washing shrinkage

64

rendered them into well fitting natural coloured swimming costume shapes with gaping rents.

At this stage accidents could happen. Fear of reprimands encouraged the ordeal of stripping in the outside lavatory, a cold lengthy process even with companionable help. When we emerged from the concrete floored W.C., Mother said, "What are you shivering for?" The tactical answer to such a stupid adult question was seized, "Combs too tight: had to take them off."

This response, with luck, might prompt a buying trip for larger sizes from our local draper in Ilford Lane. In this way success could be a mixed blessing in the 1920 slump days; frugality required clothing purchases to be made at least one size and often two sizes too big; this led to rucks at waist level, doubled over welts at sleeve and too much spare material bulging out of short trousers. We all had to 'grow into' our clothes or just 'make do' for a time. With our rapid growth it seemed to us that underwear was always too big or too tight, never just right; in winter, always tickly and with an underlying smell of damp wool, with a hint of mice.

The next torture garment, curiously named 'liberty bodice', was normally of thick cotton material with strengthened ribs, in shape rather like a waistcoat buttoned or laced at the back; difficult to remove without help and requiring close friendship or relationship if, in addition, the tight combs also needed lowering. Twin and I managed quite well, but visiting children sought maternal help whilst we smirked.

'Bodice', of course, now means the upper part of a woman's dress; formerly it was a tight fitting laced corset (another garment of torture in its own way) and originally it was simply a woman's undergarment. What 'liberty' has to do with it is hard to imagine. Possibly, if worn without one-piece combs and because it terminated at waist level, there was a certain amount of practical liberty. Anyhow, with solid fronts, liberty bodices helped keep out cold winds and household draughts. From our point of view that had other advantages; we couldn't be **sent** to bed, but had to be **put** to bed and, with luck, extort a bed-time story in the process.

Y-fronts had not arrived and, for those not promoted to long-johns (below 14/15 years old), woollen or cotton/wool mixture short underpants were used (today euphemistically named 'athletic shorts'); these had a convenient front vent, but no elastic waist. Security depended on a taped waist band intermittently secured to take braces with tabs requiring buttons sewn inside trouser waist bands. This simple, efficient system enabled underpants and trousers to be raised and lowered together.

Contrary to modern practice, we were only changed on Sundays. Compared with some children known to our parents through their London Mission work, we were fortunate; many others were sewn into whatever warm garments were available and unsewn in spring. Some Bedfordshire country children known to us were sewn into greased brown paper next to the skin and then covered by miscellaneous hand-me-downs.

In summer Twin wore thick white cotton knickers, in winter heavier navy blue, but both with elasticated legs (adult versions in pink or white were popular, named directoires). Twin soon found handkerchiefs and toffees could be accommodated above elastic level. Those privileged to receive toffee so stored in the warm were grateful for the saving in time in reducing hard toffee to delicious easily-swallowed syrup.

Winter clothing horrors did not end with underwear and remained until about eight years old in respect of leggings, requiring the adult use of button hooks. These excruciatingly awful garments were leather gaiters reaching above the knee, lined in coarse kelpy wool (advertised as 'hard wearing') secured by at least 20 buttons to clamp tightly over – in our case – already tickly socks; reaching above the knee the bare flesh suffered and, if bought to 'grow into' the lower thighs reddened. Although Twin and I tried co-operatively, we could not release the buttons for relief. Buttons were globular, rather than dished, and designed to thwart infant fingers. Like city-gent's pale grey or discreet fawn spats, our gaiters covered shoe tops and were held in place by leather straps under insteps. In wet weather the straps swelled, nickel plated buckles rusted beneath the plating and Mother, when wrestling with them progressed from red cheeks to rough action.

Shirts in summer were sometimes referred to as blouses; loose-fitting in cotton or linen with short sleeves, straight sides and enough length to cover the elasticated waist of cotton shorts; they were our favourite for comfort. In winter, fluffy grey for weekdays and white for Sundays, longer shirts with long sleeves were worn to be tucked inside the waistband. No elastic was provided; instead, two horizontal slits each side at the front and two at the back were designed to accommodate tabs from braces worn inside the shirt to be secured to buttons sewn on the inside of waistbands. A neat, clever arrangement, but difficult for fumbly fingers trying to locate the correct holes, especially at the back. I fared well with Twin's help.

Cheaper garments such as rexine helmets with ear flaps were advertised as 'fleecey-lined', a clever name for brushed cotton intended to give those unable to afford wool the impression their purchase had some association with sheep fleeces. Favoured by us because tickle free.

Long sleeved woollen jerseys of coarse wool

67

irritated bare wrists when shirts shrank. Welts always seemed tight and, by some strange law, sleeves lengthened and body parts shrank as time passed. Maybe something to do with the lack of spin dryers. Woollies dripped for a long time on the line or into bowls under the airer; often the pegs left bulges on the sleeves.

Children rarely wore leather gloves; closely knitted gloves or mitts (often, for some obscure reason, made in Arbroath). As well as tickling they retained rain as sponges and snow formed fibre secured frozen globules. Eventually in foul weather it was better to go without and simply allow them to hang from the cord joining both gloves, which had been threaded up both arms of the outergarments and around the neck.

Sleeping suits were favoured in our family; pyjamas joined at the waist, in other words. In cold bedrooms, lively or feverishly thrashing-about children would never suffer from bare midriffs. The material bore the name 'flannelette'; of heavy cotton with a slightly fluffy appearance and agreeable texture it was warm and comfortable. In most people's mind 'flannel' meant wool, the addition of 'ette' had either a French sound or the idea of miniature (and thus softer) sheep being involved in the careful manufacture. Mother fell for this advertising genius and we benefited from the smooth luxurious skin-friendly material.

Another clever name was 'art silk'; this dress fabric was shiny, showy and cheap; it also frayed around the edges, unless carefully oversewn. Many purchasers were unaware 'art' was short for 'artificial'. The synthetic material industry began with the birth of 'rayon'. Early productions creased badly, were difficult and tricky to iron without melting and casually sewn seams frayed beyond redemption. Many bachelors, acquainted with scissor trimming of ragged trouser bottoms and sleeves, found when trimming artificial silk summer shirts or scarves the resulting neatened edges only lasted a few hours before fraying into tassels.

Mother only had a few garish scarves in such material, which soon disappeared as disillusion increased. Various friends wore rayon dresses, generally in bright colours, rapidly darkening under the influence of perspiration and very tricky to wash. Shoulder pads, unlike today, were worn under the arms to protect from staining moisture, instead of above as exaggerations of shoulder angles.

*Double twins. Mother's brother, Arthur, holding me: his twin, Kathleen, holding my twin. Photograph taken in Dalkeith Road, Seven Kings, when Uncle Arthur was apprenticed to Macleans Dairy Farm, Barley Lane, Goodmayes*

# KINDERGARTEN

Grandpapa Ford, so we were told, always proclaimed that children should stay at home until seven years old because they would learn more that way by natural curiosity and experimentation. Our parents did not subscribe to this avant-garde theory and sent us to kindergarten school at $4\frac{1}{2}$ years of age.

Maybe they decided on this course because we could both read. How this came about was that Father gave me *Through the Looking Glass* and Twin *Alice's Adventures in Wonderland* (at a cost of three shillings and fourpence halfpenny per copy). The world they opened up to us meant that every adult was begged to read a chapter as our desires were insatiable. Quickly we knew the stories intimately and suddenly my twin found, to her intense delight, she could read. I was so jealous and determined to follow her achievement, I wheedled her into reading aloud to me whilst pointing to each word as she went. Somehow, I too found I could read. Supposedly the printed words hitched on to spoken words, as neither of us plodded through 'the cat is on the mat' stage, which all my children experienced.

On our first day at Miss Valance's kindergarten school the class was told to sit down as the Twins were going to read aloud from the reading book. This went off quite well and we basked in praise. The class was then asked whether anyone could remember a poem; unlike Twin I did not realise this meant any poem learnt last term and so I put up my hand, much to the surprise of Miss Valance. Without being asked I stood up to recite 'Diddly, diddly, dumtree, the cat ran up the plum tree. Give him a plum, down he'll come, diddly, diddly, dumtree.'

My sister was scarlet as she pulled me down

beside her. "Silly boy, that's not a school poem," she said with disgust.

Miss Valance thanked me kindly, whilst smothering her laugh with a cough. Later that day when told, Mother said, "Peter, you **didn't!**" She used her I-wonder-what-people-will-think look. Mother was always bothered about what folk thought about her and us; everything we did, wore or spoke was judged in that light. Appearances, reputations and conforming to the dictates of society were all important to her. Maybe just as well, Father was oblivious to such things.

In our first term, Miss Valance had ivory coloured uneven buck teeth, but by the second term displayed brilliantly white teeth uniformly receding beneath her top lip, thus destroying our previous interest in the way her lips would occasionally adhere to the original teeth until licked clear.

Sewing lessons (unisex) were held in the garden, using cards and wool which, hopefully, would become fluffy balls, the purpose of which escapes me. When, after our first session, I scrambled up from the lawn, the embryo ball was sewn to my shorts: Twin cried in shame.

Boys' shorts were always called 'knickers' by the gentlemen's outfitters authorised to sell school uniforms. Twin and I felt that somehow the designation 'boys' knickers' was slightly *infra dig* and the logic behind it, if any, was never satisfactorily explained to us; after all, girls wore hidden knickers, boys had exposed shorts covering pants; it would have made more sense to call the latter 'knickers'. Adults became irritable when questioned and we learnt to live with the inexplicable fact - shopkeepers sold 'boys' knickers'.

During that term I fell madly in love with a silky haired blonde called June and soon told her I wanted to marry her when grown up. She maturely brushed me aside, telling me kindly, even if condescendingly, not to be silly. Discussing my sadness that night in our shared bedroom, my sister comforted me by saying that June would probably change her mind later on.

A romantic view of girls lasted throughout kindergarten years, but disappeared completely at preparatory school to reappear in lecherous form at public school at the ripening age of 14.

During those first form years Gladys, a most precocious child with smooth, black hair and Madonna face, entertained us in Farmer Brown's field of rhubarb by offering to exhibit parts of herself, not normally on view, for one penny or a kiss from any boy too poor to pay. I was too poor to waste my Saturday penny on something seen every shared bath night; June was far prettier, in any case, and heroine worship breeds faithfulness, even at kindergarten.

We went to Gladys' party at the end of our first term and, for me, it ended in disaster. Suffering from a weak chest, according to various aunts, Mother made a nine inch square of thick scarlet flannel which she impregnated with camphorated oil; this was tied to my chest under an itchy woollen vest, liberty bodice and shirt. Congestion-clearing fumes were supposed to waft from chest to nose on thermal currents. Small boys playing vigorous games generate heat and soon the room smelt like a pharmacy. With so many children in such a small room it might have been possible for me to avoid being known as the boy responsible, but the string came undone during musical chairs and the hated scarlet flannel appeared below the leg of my shorts. Freezing in abject horror, I burst into tears. The slightest move would have resulted in the stinking patch sliding further.

Even at five years old acute embarrassment

72

is painful; wanting a dark hole I dared not move. Gladys' mother, bless her memory, saw the problem and, with a warmth of touch and voice I still remember, embraced me. "What's the matter, little Peter?" she asked, whilst signalling another mother for assistance. "Come into the kitchen for a cuddle." Her friend pulled the string of the scarlet horror as I buried my face in a comforting bosom to heave uncontrollable sobs.

Twin was hovering in compassionate concern and obviously prepared to sacrifice enjoyment by taking me home, but Gladys' father volunteered. The flannel was wrapped in brown paper, rapidly darkening with camphorated oil, and delivered with me to Mother. "Never mind, dear," she said as I basked on her lap before the fire, "I'll never use Aunty's silly ideas again." Before falling asleep that night I reflected how relieved I was that June was not at the party.

At Miss Valance's we learnt to chant our tables and recite the alphabet in rhythmic style, which has remained throughout our lives; particularly useful when mental blanks occur if checking spelling from the dictionary. A B C D, E F Gee - H I J K, Ellomeno Pee; Q R S Tee - U V W - X Y Z: this last stanza had no rhythm and was recited with relief at the end and thus being able to reduce our voices into guttural slides down the scale. The favourite line was 'Ellomeno Pee' and second 'Queu are esstee'. The tune was universal, natural and obvious. Anyone from my generation only has to chant the alphabet or tables as learnt at school to be joined at once by a contemporary using exactly the same intonation, rhythm and tune.

That system of learning worked well and the results lasted. However large and varied were the purchases, say, for instance, in the greengrocer's, assistants would carry a running total in their heads.

Mental arithmetic was a valued and necessary skill, as was spelling. Labels, posters and notices in shops were invariably spelt correctly, neatly written and, quite often, artistic. Giving correct change was a work of art; it was always carefully counted into the customer's hand, coin by coin. This needed more sustained day-long mental exercise than modern till operators, who simply read the printed amount of change required on the receipt.

Whilst using their powers of mental arithmetic, assistants would also engage in pleasantries. Mother would respond in a slightly restrained fashion, as she carried a running total in her head to avoid over-spending on her tight budget and also as a precaution against chicanery.

Primary education between the wars enabled folk to spell, write legibly and become proficient in mental arithmetic. The abacus was still the only mathematical aid in use, but not by Westerners, and the cumbersome mechanical adding machine only arrived after the last war. Council School children, as they were described, were launched into commerce at the age of 14 and the test given by a shopkeeper before taking a junior on trial was to check ability in the 3 Rs. Brighter children, progressing to bigger establishments, were subjected to handwriting tests as well. Even when firmly established on a counter they were, as juniors, required to have the bill of sale countersigned by a senior before any customer was expected to pay; good protection for both store and customer.

A friend of Mother's said her career in Wests' prestigious store in Cranbrook Road, Ilford, began because her teacher, knowing she was illegitimate (a serious drawback in those days), had drummed into her the importance of the 3 Rs, plus personal deportment. In middle age she still walked with a regal stance which Twin and I found rather daunting and reminiscent of austere shopwalkers descending on active small children threatening to become a nuisance in the hardware department. These feelings faded rapidly when we discovered she liked helping us with our arithmetic homework and was extremely good at it and patient in explaining.

When Mother stood at the gate to wave as she turned the corner, after enjoying an evening with our family, she always said, admiringly, "What a wonderfully straight back she has!"

When walking in hand-linked crocodile to South Park for recreation and ball games once a week, we were ordered to straighten shoulders, lift our feet instead of shuffling, and hold heads up. Twin and I would reduce ourselves to giggles in the garden during holidays by exaggerating both Miss Valance's tone of voice and physical actions involved.

Frequent injunctions from teachers, parents, friends and relatives were ... "Take your hands out of your pockets... Raise your cap to that lady... Stand up when a lady comes into the room... Give your seat to that lady... Open the door for Aunty... Don't start eating until we've all been served... Take your elbows off the table... No cake until you've finished your bread and butter... Children should be seen and not heard... Stop fiddling, sit up straight and take your hands off the table... Carry that bag for your mother... Pass the sauce round before you help yourself... Offer your sister first choice... Keep quiet and only speak when you're spoken to... Stand up straight when I'm talking to you... Don't be cheeky, you do it because I say so, and that's that!"

These phrases were so familiar we knew they were coming before they were uttered. They seem to have lasted throughout life, but are not recognised in their effects these days. Women's Lib may have something to do with it; I struggled to my feet from a deep chair recently when a charming woman in her early thirties entered the room. "Don't go yet," she said. Later that evening, when opening the door to the darkened hall and standing aside to let her go first, she said, "You're not frightened of the dark at your age, surely?" A contemporary of mine offered his seat to a young woman in the Underground this year. "Don't be so... patronizing," said she, as she continued to stand.

In the early 20th century all classes understood, appreciated and responded to good manners. If an adult reprimanded a child for lack of manners and the parent was there, the child would receive another reprimand from the parent. Nobody would dream of saying, "How dare you talk to my child like that?" It would more likely be, "I'm so sorry, I'll deal with him later."

In St Andrew's Church, The Drive, Ilford, Mother took us to a special service one day. I forgot to take my cap off on entering. A large imposing sidesman with mutton-chop whiskers sailed down the aisle like a man o' war, grabbed my cap, plus several hairs, and thrust it into Mother's hands with a hiss of disapproval. Instead of being cross at his roughness, she was contrite at my lack of manners. Having been reminded of my manners by the sidesman I was more careful for a few days.

One morning in class the angelic June entered the room after 'being excused' and I felt both comfortable and gallant as I stood up, and aggrieved when Miss Valance told me to sit down. The object of my love swept past with her nose in the air to resume her spelling cards oblivious of passionate emotions aroused in the second row. "You're not meant to stand up for **everybody**," whispered Twin. "Only for grown-ups and **important** people."

At that stage the most important person in my life was the unattainable June, with golden locks draping her pedestal. Life was very unfair.

76

There was an end of term activity which we rehearsed for several weeks. Mothers had to provide costumes resembling rabbits; to my delight, I was chosen as a male rabbit to hold hands with June, the 'leading lady' rabbit in order to sing a song. Rehearsals were bliss as my hot grubby hands clasped her cool fingers. I targeted my singing at her right ear, but she raised her blue eyes towards the stained glass panels (so popular then for display above main windows) and seemed oblivious to my emotions pouring out in song concerning buttercups, daisies and whispering breezes of evening. With tresses flowing over her shoulders, she tossed her head in disdain and slipped her fingers from my ardent, sticky grasp.

Instinctively responding to the anguish in my heart and showing mature understanding of the need for a positive outlook, Twin said, "You look soppy when you're singing with June." For once, I had no answer.

Our parents at the time were heavily into the Plymouth Brethren denomination and, when they heard we were to appear in a 'theatrical' event at school, withdrew us forthwith, because acting was 'of the Devil'. A horrible little boy called Nigel, with permanent and visible catarrh, took my part and held June's hand. Because it was 'worldly' we did not even go to the end of term show.

Twin and I were the only pupils to receive boxes of chocolates (extremely rare as gifts for children) from Miss Valance and her mother after the show. I would still have preferred June's cool hand in mine, singing in shared song, to any chocolate compensation, even if from the revered Miss Valance.

Whether she eventually married, or her supportive mother died, or economics eventually torpedoed the venture, I cannot recall and was probably not told, in any case. Maybe our parents decided we were not 'getting on' or ought to be challenged. Whatever it was, kindergarten life, with all its pleasures and gentle learning, came to an end.

Twin was sent to St Winifred's College for Girls in nearby Goodmayes: we never found out why a small private school should have been named after a 7th century patron saint of north Wales – possibly because she was a virgin or maybe the original founder came from Wales. School uniforms were obligatory – brown gym slips and cream blouses. A good walking advertisement for the school and, for parents, a head start in the Jones' race!

I was taken by Mother to see Mr Taylor, Headmaster of Clark's Modern School for Boys (known, rather superiorly, as Clark's College) at 83 Cranbrook Road, Ilford: a pleasant, thin-lipped man with fascinating dried spittle in his mouth corners.

Mother explained my kindergarten beginnings and her desire to see me progress. She also emphasised for both our benefits that her husband had worked out the financial side and they were prepared to make sacrifices (another meaningful look to me) so that both their children could be well educated. To make the point that they were serious and able to make such noble personal deprivations, she mentioned St Winifred's College for Girls. To underline parental support and ambition, she repeated, "We want to see him progress."

This underlying and subtle implication that I was not fulfilling expectations was, I am sure, intended for my benefit and as a spur; Mr Taylor, however, detected the undercurrents and said abruptly, "Stand up, Ford." I was accustomed to being called Peter and was therefore slow to respond. Mother prodded me to my feet as he fixed me with a stern expression, "Tell me, Ford, what are four fours?"

78

After a long moment of horror under his cold gaze on my reddening face I blurted out, "Nine."

"Oh, Peter!" said Mother.

"Form 1B, I think," said Mr Taylor.

"My husband will want to know how many boys are in that class."

"Only three," he said, with a note of thankfulness in his voice. Mother seemed pleased at this prospect of individual attention, unaware it was the dolts' class.

The strain on the family purse in buying a brown blazer, horizontally striped brown and white tie and school cap from Pursers in Cranbrook Road, was lost on me at the time, but I remember an anxious air around Mother during earnest discussions in the shop about minimum numbers of socks, shirts and football shorts required. The final financial blow came when she found that special flexible dipping pen nibs were needed in order to learn the copperplate writing for which Clark's was well known.

That night, with bedroom door ajar, we listened to the long and serious discussion coming from under the dining room door as our parents worked out the exact cost, to the penny, of paying for our education. There was an atmosphere in the home which, at least for a time, motivated us to merit their sacrifice for us. After one term I was promoted to 1A and came third out of twelve, instead of first out of three.

Apart from enjoyable reading lessons and the embarrassment of having to read out compositions written as homework, all I can remember of academic standards is the fuss made about hand writing loops and hooks, and the importance of wiping the copper coloured nibs with blotting paper to avoid rusting and ruining the necessary flexibility needed for thick downstrokes and thin upstrokes.

Every desk was equipped with a sunken inkwell, filled every day by a sour faced domestic. By half term sludge accumulated, a great impediment in making thin strokes.

Socially, I learnt many interesting new words to share with my sister and, more privately, several ingenious ways of 'being excused' in what seemed at that time an endless length of white porcelain urinal with permanent flush and a long row of careless and often ambitious neighbours, mostly bent on demonstrating powers of liquid expression in terms of elevation.

The acquisition of a 'common' accent was, however, the deciding factor in being withdrawn in favour of Park School, near the Wash in Cranbrook Road; a preparatory school of high reputation for manners and, as Mother said, "Nice boys".

Today it sounds unforgivably snobby even to think accent is important, but in the 20s it was, especially in connection with careers above the manual worker level. People could even distinguish between an Oxford or Cambridge University accent. Oxford was supposed to have a languid drawl and Cambridge a softer, more clipped ending to words. I had neither!

# PARK SCHOOL

Park School, long since turned into flats, was owned and managed by a music graduate, Mr Chas. Hughes, ably supported by his wife.

The fees were more than our family budget could manage; £4 per term or £5 with lunches. Although Mr Hughes did not offer scholarships, he was keen to recruit boys with singing potential. I was blessed with a good voice and, after preliminary and optimistic discussions between Head and parents, an interview and voice trial was arranged.

"Sing 'la la' to this tune," he said, and I obliged. "Sing a verse of any hymn." I sang 'There is a green hill far away' as Mr Hughes joined in on the piano.

"Hmm," he said, "in the right key. Follow these notes until you cannot go any higher." I was surprised how high I could go. Mr Hughes turned to Mother and said, "Excuse me a moment, I'd like my wife to give her opinion." Mrs Hughes was a comfortable, competent woman, who listened attentively to a repeat performance. As we left, she ruffled my hair pleasantly.

A few days later, Twin and I listened from the kitchen as Father discussed with Mother a letter saying that, in view of my singing potential and because Mrs Hughes was particularly keen, they would accept me as a pupil and would not charge for school lunches. There was great rejoicing as the £1 saved enabled me to go to Park School.

Sadly, shortly afterwards Mrs Hughes died very suddenly, but bless his heart, Mr Hughes was faithful to her wishes and I spent all my preparatory school days enjoying free lunches.

Another anxious visit was paid to the school outfitters; this time it was black blazers for every-

81

day use with starched white collars and black and white striped ties. For special events we had 'bum-freezer' single breasted jackets with long trousers in grey and black stripes. To complete the misery we wore stiff white Eton collars, as per Billy Bunter. The jackets were cut away at the back, hence the nickname, and the trousers had inch and a half turn-ups which, by clever manipulation, could be turned into false turn-ups one inch longer and therefore cope with a term's growth. People on tight budgets, such as ours, managed another term by abolishing the turn-up altogether.

The first change for the better came when we were allowed to wear blazers for all events, providing we had the Eton collar worn on the out-side. Final release from misery came when grey shorts and black blazers, with smaller stiff white collars worn inside the jacket, were authorised by Headmaster's edict.

Even so, I came in for a certain amount of good natured barracking on the bus to school every day, especially when the bus conductor caught me licking a handkerchief to wipe off the dirty fingerprints on my Eton collar which had shown up in the reflection from the front window of the bus and had been missed by Mother's eagle eye in the dim light of dawn.

Stiff white collars were the fashion for all ages of males; collar laundries called weekly with hardened cardboard boxes in which soiled collars were placed to be brought back in pristine condition. Most laundry firms promised to replace worn, frayed collars with new, at no extra charge. Sometimes they were slow so to do and I recall many occasions when the frayed portions were stiffly starched into saw teeth as a torture weapon for chin and neck.

Those unwilling to use cotton starched collars could buy white celluloid collars and shirt cuffs which, in theory, only needed washing with soap and water to retain their original appearance, but which, in practice, slowly turned yellow with the action of skin oil. I learnt from adult comments that such do-it-yourself smartness was a mark of inferior status!

The piano tuner we loved because he concluded his sessions with swingy popular tunes utilizing every note on the key board, wore white, turning to yellow, cuffs and collars. When we jumped up and down and clapped in rhythm, he was inspired to liven up the test piece with such vigour the celluloid cuffs shot out to overlap his sleeve ends; on one occasion his front collar stud broke loose and the collar sprang against his cheek, where it was ignored as the piano rocked to his enthusiasm and the floor bounced under our dancing.

The drawing room smelt of dust when he left. We knew Mother listened from the dining room, with his fee ready to accompany her warm words of farewell. Smiling at each other in anticipation, we heard the invariable comment, "What a nice man; what a pity his wife doesn't give him **proper** collars and cuffs."

One day he brought a packed lunch of the thickest sandwiches we had ever seen, full of cheese and onion rings, with bread an inch thick on both sides; he used both hands and a wide gape in order to consume with obvious relish. Mother provided a cup of strong tea and in polite conversation learnt he was a widower now 'doing for himself'. From then on he not only had tea, but often gingerbread or raspberry buns and, sometimes, a few extra in a bag for later on.

He made such a proficient job of tuning our old wooden framed piano that Father recommended him to Mr Hughes for the ramshackle, note-missing and decrepit piano used in the assembly room at Park

School. Nothing came of it and more and more notes ceased to sound: Mr Hughes compensated by using more volume and spread of his large hands.

The Park School day began with what was then called 'Swedish Drill', but later Physical Jerks. In all weathers, except heavy rain or snow, we performed exercises on a concrete back yard, led by the unfortunate duty master.

"In, out, in, out, up, down, up, down." Some masters became breathless before others and often we judged their mood by the speed set. 'Slow' meant we might in class be allowed to read quietly or copy text book paragraphs; 'fairly fast' indicated the ominous introduction of a new subject or Latin declension (we began Latin in the first form); 'very fast' presaged a bad-tempered verbal spelling test or, as far as I was concerned, the dreaded mental arithmetic test with an irritable master pacing the rows whilst swinging the chalk eraser.

After the demise of the Billy Bunter uniforms we wore grey flannel shorts and, at drill when sitting on our heels, knees were stretched and exposed; one particularly vicious and irritable master on a 'very fast' morning came along the row, stopped by me and, using more volume than usual, shouted, "Ford, your knees are disgustingly filthy."

From then on the spittle moistened handker-chief on the bus was used for both starched collar and grubby knees. Mother soon noticed the messy linen and linked this to the causes; after that I had to scrub my knees with a soaped loofah every night.

Private prep school masters were badly paid in the 20s, despite often being graduates. One in particular had a bedroom intended for a servant on the top floor of Park School. I was despatched one day to collect a book for him and was amazed at the bare boards and miserable bed on black iron legs. A rickety chair lolled toward the few garments hanging sadly on a rod balanced on the picture rails in the corner; there was an overwhelming smell of stale sweat and socks. The suit he wore for class was shiny and smelly; cuffs were frayed and sometimes trimmed in class with scissors; turn-ups worn through by constant dragging because nobody had offered to shorten his trousers, hung in gaping loops behind his heels. He also looked permanently hungry.

Somehow Mother heard of this and invited him to afternoon tea one Sunday. I was sent to the corner to meet and usher him, but hardly recognised the smart man striking me dumb with his "Hello, Peter." Christian names were only for family use. Even special school friends used surnames or nicknames based thereon: Christian names were sissy.

My transformed master was plied with ham sandwiches and cakes until he had to lean back in the chair to make room for digestion to begin. Later he was pampered with paper bags full of home-made buns (annoying me as I sensed personal deprivation). Somehow Mother manoeuvred conversation to the subject of laundry and renovation, only to hear there was no problem. This shook my faith in the absolute integrity of schoolmasters.

"Peter will see you to the corner," said Mother, much to my distress and horror. This seemed to me like a tightrope across the chasm between master and pupil.

"Good evening, sir," I said at the pillar box and, to my astonishment, Mr Cocks shook my hand, saying, "Good evening, Peter, and thank you."

I knew I had fallen off the tightrope when, next day, he cuffed me round the ear for failing to give the correct Latin for 'thou wilt love': I think I gave him 'thou hast loved' - thus summing up what can happen with a forced unnatural relationship imposed from above, even if it develops properly.

Thus was my faith concerning the benefits and pleasures of personal relationships with masters stifled.

Never again at Park School was I called Peter and, even when promoted to charge of the break-time tuck shop, an honourable position of trust, rewarded with broken chocolate bars, I was still, coldly, Ford. Just once Mother's kindness had a positive outcome when we played a local school at cricket and, in order to finish in one day, we continued into early evening. My job was to dispense lime juice; most boys had the required tuppence, except me. It was a hot afternoon, I had lugged the heavy case of lime juice essence to the P.L.A. playing fields, filled and carried large glass bottles of water and was now selling refreshment to the wealthy, whilst resigning myself to plain water. Mr Cocks, with more perception than I had credited him with, said, "Help yourself, Ford, and give me a glass at the same time." Maybe Mother's home-made cakes had had a beneficial effect after all!

Corporal punishment, as far as I recall, was not even a phrase in general use. Masters hit us around the head or pulled short hairs above the ears and twisted as well, if so inclined or provoked, as they would claim. Headmasters caned our bottoms as a matter of course. Parents were not consulted or informed, in fact we generally avoided any mention of such things at home; red rimmed eyes were explained as passing buses blinding us with dust. Admission of chastisement at school would result in a repeat performance at home. "We are not sacrificing all that money on your schooling to have you fooling about and wasting it."

Masters would often say, "You're wasting your parents' money, so PAY ATTENTION!"

A tram conductor, noticing my school uniform and lack of manners, prodded my shoulder, saying loudly, "Your parents, sonny boy, are spending a lot of money for you to be taught manners - GET UP and give this lady your seat." I did so at once, and felt no resentment, only guilt at such a well 'hammered in' courtesy being neglected by me, the privileged one.

I cannot recall being aware of other people's envy of private schooling, but many times felt their sense of knowing exactly what such expense should produce in the way of manners and of being judged, generally good temperedly, for any lack on my part. It is possible that when class distinctions were clearly defined, as they were in the 20s, and barriers between them rarely breached - envy was less than that created by extreme politicians of today in this age of Christian names, relative affluence and supposed equality of opportunity. Maybe some lack-lustre, uninspiring and often failed political systems only exist on greed, envy and hatred fanned by vicious sounds from out of office politicians.

Successful people were held up to us, in the 20s, as being there to emulate; any suggestion that they were lucky or specially privileged was met with, "There's nothing to stop you getting to the top if you work hard enough".

The most enjoyable times at Park School were daily music lessons. We sang popular songs (not allowed at home) as a warm up and then practised operettas for the end of term concert.

Donald, a platinum blond boy with a superb voice generally had the main part, which normally made all the mothers dewy-eyed at such an angelic presentation. I was the next best. My most difficult part was as Pied Piper, with many solos, and as an added hazard, learning to play a tin whistle, supposed to be played in a lively fashion whilst dancing at the head of the procession of rats and children. I just about managed to learn the simple tune, but could only play it at half speed and, instead of dancing, only managed a solemn shuffle. Fingering needed concentration, as did avoidance of treading on the raised toes of a much adapted jester's costume, hired locally as the nearest available style to the Pied Piper (according to Ilford's current theatrical expertise).

Every now and then it was necessary to stop the procession to sing another song; a relief only spoilt by the long time it then took to place fingers over the correct holes on the whistle to lead a joyful, erratic column of children trying not to laugh. As it was good business for the school to include every child in these concerts, thus ensuring a maximum attendance of parents, relatives and friends, it meant an extremely long cavalcade stopping and starting according to the ripples begun by those nearest the whistle. Lack of concentration resulted in gaps to be filled by leaps and bounds, reminiscent of a badly-played concertina.

Parents were intended to react with sentimental 'ooh-aahs', but I'm afraid became helpless with 'ha-has' at every solemn tin whistle led progression at funereal speed. I was puzzled and hurt, but Twin explained it was my serious and troubled expression which made them laugh, not my jerky walk and lack of musical ability. Anyhow, the Headmaster presented me with the nickel plated whistle later that week.

Near Cranbrook Park was a large house filled with theatrical costumes for hire and my outfit had to be returned there in due course. I was taken, together with the bright green and yellow costume, to hand them back. The fusty rooms, full of weird props and ornate clothing were my first introductions to and awareness of various odours attached to the human body under stress. The only personal freshness aids available in the 1920s seemed to be soap and water, talcum powder and perfume (we called it scent) liberally spread or splashed. When female guests arrived, probably by bus or tram and a long walk, they were shown into Mother's bedroom to freshen up; this included powder puffing the face, dabbing scent strategically, but sometimes only partially effectively (Californian Poppy was one brand we recognised by its sharp smell) and then entering the living room smelling fresh or, at least, newly camouflaged. Clothing in cupboards, wardrobes and especially in choir vestries soon lost imparted fragrance and reverted.

The other end-of-term concert I remember vividly was towards the conclusion of my time at Park School, when we performed a musical version of *Julius Caesar* (our Headmaster favoured the hard C - Kaesar). Many parents were misled until the the second chorus established the Roman connection. I was chosen for the part of Caesar. All told, this entailed one hour of solos; not too daunting, except for the problems with the too-large silvered *papier maché* helmet the theatrical costumier assured us would be perfectly adequate if stuffed with newspaper. It was so for rehearsals, but on the big night, a combination of nervous strain, spotlights and audience body heat caused humidity and temperature levels to rise inside the helmet, which then slowly descended, not only over my ears, but my eyes also. Having practised dramatic gestures as extra emphasis in forceful passages, I had not anticipated costume troubles, but having had it drummed into us that on stage you must **keep going**, I continued singing in the equivalent of a dew moistened conch shell. Once again and unintentionally, I helped to 'make' the evening for parents in danger of boredom.

In those days, boredom concerning anything to do with paying for education was a challenging thought. If 'they', i.e. those we are paying, cannot do better than that, then what is the point of sacrificing so much of our hard earned income?

Mr Chas. Hughes had the remarkable ability of making the most unlikely boys sing like angels. A great asset in those competitive and slump threatening days; any child who could be shown to have some sort of talent would stand a chance of earning a living, even if the talent was only in singing and this was worth struggling for, come what may. After all, there were a few choral scholarships available for the gifted.

One of Mr Hughes' most dramatic and effective teaching gestures was to tap his forehead whilst pounding out the melody with one hand on the piano and singing in a peculiar high pitched flutelike voice,"Sing in your **foreheads**, sing in your **foreheads.**" Somehow, without understanding the technique, we grasped the idea and projected our voices from the top of our heads, instead of rasping from the throat or droning through the nose.

Many boys subsequently joined parish church choirs. I longed to, but also, Plymouth Brethren (by convictions I never fully understood) had no choirs. I can, however, remember one evening service when an Elder announced, "Our sister Mabel will now render praise to the Lord in spiritual song." This was also known as singing the gospel and it seemed a vibrato effect was essential. My sister and I, impressed by the shaking head and wobbly hat, practised in the safety of our bedroom until helpless with giggles.

When Latin progressed to second form level we understood why the ivory stop on Father's foot-pedal Bell harmonium, which made all notes pulsate, was labelled *Vox humana*; rarely used by him, because if his pedal power waned through weariness, the fading sounds became syncopated and staccato

90

as bellows sagged and sighed in sad response.

Although attaining a certain notoriety in singing, that was all. School reports, even making due allowance for the need to keep parents paying fees reasonably happily, were mainly of the 'should concentrate more, could do better if he tried' variety; carefully chosen remarks implying the excellence of the tuition offered and failings of pupils, easily corrected by hard pressed parents continuing to pay whilst trying to survive and maintain standards in depression years.

Such dreaded documents were gone through by parents with me sitting in misery before them. During regrettable regular sessions, resolves were made to be more worthy of the sacrifices in future. I now know these were very real sacrifices in such desperate slump years as we had in the 20s with futures insecure, indefinite and overshadowed with an ever looming spectre of unemployment with minimal unemployment hand-outs and the crushing fear of falling into debt.

Our form master, probably from psychological motives, had the sadistic habit of reading out the end of term reports from his podium, before handing them to us in envelopes carefully licked, sealed and rubbed with bitten thumb nail along the edge, which we knew, without being told, was to make sure that no opening or altering took place on the way home. We guessed he had overheard various whispered conversations behind the Tuck Shop when we suggested ways of altering position-in-class figures and adding 'very' in front of 'fair' or 'good' or, as one boy (who became a famous doctor) proposed, adding 'not' after the 'could' of 'could try harder'.

The maths master found in me an object of derision and supposedly imagined others would avoid my degradation in having to repeat after a stupid mistake was questioned, "Because I'm a fool, sir!"

91

Each word was punctuated by him with a slap to the side of my head. Any hesitation resulted in the short hairs over the ears being pulled. On one occasion I dissolved into tears and hated him for inflicting such indignity.

The inborn respect for any form of authority and awareness of parental sacrifices on my behalf meant such humiliating events were never disclosed to parents or friends. An open door for sadistic masters to enter! Better to keep the head down during maths lessons, nursing a fear-paralysed brain vaguely sensing with relief that previous outbursts of tears were actually preventing even that hated man from having another go at me.

Not all masters were hated, the teacher we all loved was tall and angular with a distressing eye affliction necessitating holding printed matter a few inches from his face whilst his eyes flickering rapidly from side to side. He was witty, kind and avuncular and rode a Norton motor cycle with huge sidecar, which he allowed us to sit on in the cycle shed. Alas, he did not stay more than two terms. A measure of the affection we had for him can be seen in that we had no nickname for him, even though his surname was probably one of the most unfortunate any schoolmaster could own -Daubieballs!

# ST WINIFRED'S

Sport, we were told, built our characters and imbued us with team spirit. Wednesday afternoons and, occasionally much to our disgust, Saturdays for special inter-school matches were sacrosanct.

When clearing out a trunk recently I came across my tatty first eleven cap badge, which only evoked miserable memories of enforced cricket, hockey and football (always called 'footer', never 'soccer'). I hated the smell of wintry grass crushed into mud and the continual shouts of 'pass, pass', especially as I was always inside right and had to pass to the centre forward who generally missed and blamed me, probably rightly, for a slovenly pass.

The most memorable goal I scored was when, by luck, I sent the football inaccurately towards the goal and a loose nail from a worn stud burst it with a loud report, as the collapsed leather flopped into goal at 30° off my line of kick. The referee allowed the goal. After all, there was nothing in the rules about having air in the ball and I enjoyed the 'Well played, Ford'. I tried to disguise pleasure when we heard no spare ball was available and we could go home.

Hockey was slightly more enjoyable as it seemed to me easier to hit a ball with a cunningly designed stick, also the schools we played seemed to be far less skilled and, when playing 'away', the changing rooms were better appointed and lemon slices and drinks lavish compared with ours. My enthusiasm waned somewhat when I was laid off games for three weeks, having been knocked out by a ball on my forehead. For the first time, when receiving solicitous ministrations from the master in charge, I realised schoolmasters were actually human and, when accompanied home on the bus with an egg-sized lump, I felt as if being

*Park School's Sports Day winners, Summer, 1932. Author extreme right, clutching two left handed boxing gloves*

cherished by a favourite uncle.

On Monday, however, I determined on my way to school not to expect any special treatment, in view of the memory of normality returning shortly after the master who had come to tea. I was not wrong in my lack of expectation as, during 'notices' he reported we had won the hockey match on Saturday, despite a promising member of the team being knocked out by dreamily getting in the way of a rising ball!

He was referee at the next match in which I played and unintentionally I hit his shin with full force. He crumpled in agony and I felt no remorse at the time, as it seemed to me and Twin during later soul-baring discussion that this might well be an example of Biblical 'just retribution'.

We detected our parents were not particularly impressed by games. Scraped up money was wasted and could have been better used academically. This was contrary to the general view, which regarded excellence in sport as laudable as in the field of learning. They did, however, come to Sports Days, even though avoiding inter-school matches. The hated master always appeared in immaculate cream flannels and striped college blazer, flourishing a megaphone to announce and organise events. I invariably won the odd types of events - egg and spoon, sack and three-legged race. The only prize I remember clearly was a pair of boxing gloves, which turned out to be two left-hand gloves. Father sportingly called at the sports shop in Cranbrook Road to enquire whether they had two right hand gloves in stock, which after careful search they said they hadn't and so I was relieved of the frightening prospect of finding sparring partners.

The encouraging outcome was that I realised my father was sympathetic to disappointments and not solely a disciplinarian dispensing chastisement (sometimes corporal) and edicts. Not being able to launch myself into boxing as a hobby was an added comfort and also consolation for a useless prize. A cementing of my feeling that Father was actually as human as other boys' fathers appeared to be came at the end of a Sports Day when fathers were megaphoned to enter the Fathers' Race for a hundred yard sprint. Several were members of the local cricket team and well used to sports clothing and therefore suitably dressed in white open-necked shirts, belted (not braced) grey flannels and shoes with anti-skid patterned soles. Father, who possessed no sports clothes and would never have wasted money on such casual requirements, was wearing his usual business grey suit, trousers held up by braces and white shirt with stiff collar and formal navy blue spotted tie.

As the megaphone pleaded with fathers to be 'good sports' and join in, Mother said, "Come on, Laurie, you can run fast." There was a pause, during which I prayed he would not be tempted to compete.

"Hmm," mused Father, "I used to be very fast at school." I prayed desperately for intervention, rashly promising God instant reforms.

"Go on, Laurie, go on," urged Mother.

With bitter thoughts about God not bothering to answer earnest prayers and blushes of doom-laden apprehensions from neck to cheeks, I watched as he removed jacket, waistcoat and loose change from trouser pockets and walked to the starting line. He was the only one wearing braces and black leather soled Gibson shoes and the only one not included in the friendly banter of the more suitably clad fathers on the starting line, most of whom were active members of the Ilford cricket, tennis and rowing clubs (too worldly for us Plymouth Brethren).

With an overwhelming premonition of disaster and failure and a yearning to be mature enough to help and advise my betters, I stood in misery with an expression Mother read on my face. "Your father always walks very fast and his sisters often told me

95

he was the fastest runner in the family." Mother's loyal optimism only increased my sense of forthcoming humiliation.

The starting pistol fired. Father was quick off the mark and, initially, his sisters' description seemed apposite; unfortunately his shiny leather soles on grass were no match for those wearing speciality soles and half way along the agonisingly long track he fell behind to come in last, having expended more of himself than all the rest of them. Feeling he had won the race by sheer effort, I wept within, not from shame at his un-athletic attire or appearance, but because after such supreme striving to please Mother and me, he had come in last.

Instead of a bright red face, as had the others, his was deathly pale. I longed to hold his hand in an effort to transmit the feelings I had, but lacked the courage of maturity. On that day Father became not only human and fallible, but also lovable and somebody to cherish and protect, if only I knew how.

Twin's school avoided all such parental traumas and she seemed to live a comfortable and uncomplicated life at St Winifred's College for Girls, Broomfield Road, Goodmayes. It was always **my** problems, embarrassments, failures, difficulties and moderate successes we discussed, never hers. Unlike mine, her handwriting was neat, her spelling reliable, her arithmetic competent, her deportment immaculate and her social graces mature and confident; every trait, in fact, which encouraged hard-up parents to forego expensive holidays for such a worthy child and an ideal, hopefully long-stay pupil in the eyes of a headmistress proprietor with cash-flow problems.

At that time I was twelve inches shorter than Twin and, had she not been such a loyal champion of her brother, I would have been convinced of being inferior in every way. Strangely enough, my advice was regularly sought and sometimes taken by her.

97

Between the wars and no doubt after World War II for a time, one rarely asked the advice of parents on personal matters. Mateyness between parents and children had not yet arrived in our circles. Nevertheless, love, compassion, concern and family loyalty were strong emotions, but sharing childish problems, with only a few exceptions, were predictably likely to result in gentle censure, followed by firm lectures on morals and ethics.

"It's no good asking **them**, you know what they'll say," was a frequent phrase in our conversations. In some ways, of course, a compliment to efficient parental teaching and example.

Having found out that my bus ticket entitled me to one more stop on the 145 route and that St Winifred's at the end of that stop had one more afternoon class than Park School, I would use the facility to wait outside Twin's school, sitting on the stone parapet of the front garden wall, enjoying the sickly sweet smells of privet blossom and the sing-song responses of pupils in the front room wafted to me on the interior smells of india rubber, leather satchels, tired end-of-day gym slips and fading lavender water from the sharp-voiced form mistress.

It was a pampered and privileged feeling to be free from school oppression, whilst others were still suffering. Disclosure of this arrangement to parents was never contemplated; we knew it would involve earnest discussions concerning whether the **boy's** school was giving full value for money as against the **girl's**. In overheard conversations our parents rarely used our names... understandable, I suppose, as they received unexpectedly two instead of one).

We walked the mile home, talking first about the injustices of the day and then planning what we would do during the holiday down at the farm.

Miss Whitaker, the headmistress, was a very fair tartar, whose word was law and never challenged because of her impartial judgements. Instead of end of term concerts she favoured Gym Displays in the local church hall. This was before the days of eurhythmics and their various offspring and was considered very modern and healthy for mind and body; possibly an infection from Scandinavia and Germany and the upsurge of naturism generally. Not that St Winifred's provided any display of bare flesh; the marching, jumping and gyrating of girls from 6 to 16 years was performed without eroticism in gym slips and blouses.

"My word," said Mother to a neighbour, "some of those seniors are very well developed." Twin and I were not quite sure what this meant, but agreed that some of the prefects were rather floppy with what was euphemistically called 'puppy fat'.

The closing item was always the school choir singing what I regarded as soppy songs with sissy words, extolling the virtues of flowers, birds and happy fauns gambolling through flower bedecked meadows. I thought the thin and occasionally strident voices compared rather badly with boys. Vaunting this view caused a row between Twin and me on the walk home and required a long halt for violent altercation. On reaching our gate she realised her raincoat, in the heat of the moment, had been left on a chestnut paling fence. United in disaster, dreading consternation at home for the need to find more money for a new raincoat and the consequent punishment meted out to us, we rushed back, only to find the coat had gone.

Twin panicked and did not, for once, shrug off physical comfort, as I held her arm. "We can say it was stolen," I said in desperation and shaky defiance of moral laws. When we arrived home, there, on the doorstep was a neighbour saying 'goodbye' to Mother, who was holding the raincoat and offering profuse thanks for good neighbourliness. "If you do that again," scolded Mother to Twin, "you'll have to get wet. I can't afford another."

Such events gave us a working knowledge of the value of money and the impossibility of raising extra cash to cover disasters in a stretched domestic economy.

The prim, correct Miss Whitaker retired, and the school was bought by Miss Murphy, a charming, friendly and forthcoming Irishwoman. Twin blossomed yet more under her leadership. "Miss Murphy says this... Miss Murphy says that... Miss Murphy was really pleased with me... Miss Murphy says I've done really well", were comments which began to pall somewhat.

Undoubtedly parents and pupils were pleased with her leadership and the school progressed further. Then came the dreaded School Certificate examinations. Twin, we were assured, would sail through them, as indeed she would have, had not Miss Murphy spent the entrance fee elsewhere, only to confide in parents at the last minute that the exam could not take place. She was so well liked that, despite the bitter disappointment and consequent problems, no parent was prepared to take her to court. The school closed at the end of term and the large, double-fronted house reverted to living accommodation.

Twin ended her schooling without certification. To give the wretched headmistress/proprietor her due, she wrote a reference for my sister admitting the financial fiasco and her incompetence and expressing an opinion, based on her own M.A.(Cantab) as to my sister's prospects had she been able to sit the examination. This enabled Twin eventually, and without School Certificate, to enrol for and obtain her S.R.N. at Guy's Hospital.

So awful was the prospect of going to law, so dreadful the consequences and so crippling the victim's burden if convicted nobody in our so-called and labelled middle class would rush into litigation unless convinced the offender was an absolute shyster and deserving punishment.

"Miss Murphy was a sweet woman" (as we heard Mother say and Twin confirmed between sobs) "and the less said, soonest mended."

All parents agreed with these sentiments, despite financial and academic hardships experienced. Even when taking account of grim realities, one could postulate it was a kinder, more tolerant world between the wars. Litigious fever from America had not yet reached our shores.

*Twin, Mother and me beside the garage Father drove through with his first car. Note the unequal size of the twins, 1934*

# SUNDAYS

One constraint on our social lives between the wars was class boundaries over which one never crossed. Professional people made friends with those of equal status, middle classes carefully graded by unwritten laws, stayed within their own bounds and the working classes 'knew their place'. Each strata had several levels within it, for instance, shopkeepers were 'in trade' and therefore lower middle class, whereas bank managers were upper middle class and clerks were in a transition stage from lower to whatever their skills or enterprise led them in higher grades.

We were never taught these distinctions in so many words, but rather sensed them by attitudes, manners, tone of voice or accent. For instance, when talking to a professional man, Mother's accent would become more genteel; speaking to a member of the working class she used a more patronising, authoritative tone. This was automatic and a universal product of the clear-cut class divisions of the time. To be fair, it is easier to understand what seems so odious if the social mores, habits, appearances, dress, language, behaviour, outlook and property of each is taken into account and due allowance made for the vast gulfs separating each person's 'station in life', in those days.

To their credit, in Plymouth Brethren circles social barriers were much less firmly defined, if at all. We entertained professional folk in our humble home without any pretentious claims from our parents. Those whom many would have called uncouth and not suitable to mix with were offered hospitality and friendship at all times; it was only in later years we learnt that this attitude was unusual.

In our narrow religious world, the only barrier recognised as relevant in our social lives was that of

102

Faith. Whatever the status, whether below, equal to or above ours, if folk were 'believers' we mixed socially without question. Worldly, normally accepted criteria were, of course, recognised by our parents and, indeed, sympathised with to a certain extent, but because of personal conviction based upon Evangelical 'Brethren's' teaching from infancy, were dismissed out of hand as contrary to their understanding of the Scriptures. Maybe this was a Christianised *laager* approach to life, but at least it inculcated an amount of respect for and recognition of moral, ethical and religious views and differences of opinion held by so many people we met.

If acquaintances were not Christian (i.e. not practising, professing members of a church, chapel or assembly approved by the Brethren) then, according to our father, they were 'worldly' and that was that. No social contact allowed!

As we were not permitted to go to the cinema (called 'pictures' then) and had no radio (wireless) and would never go to a theatre because that was 'of the devil', we would probably have been boring guests to anybody other than fellow Plymouth Brethren anyway. Within such harsh sounding confines we did, in fact, live full social lives. Several characters from the local Assembly Hall were regular and colourful visitors.

Mr Lepine, an important looking local preacher, sported fluffy mutton chop whiskers, a wing collar and diamond studded cravat, which pulsated with the intensity of his preaching voice. In common with most Plymouth Brethren, he was self-taught from the Scriptures and therefore tended to view personally preferred and selected texts as literally true in every detail which supported his own views. His sing-song soporific voice was periodically punctuated with vigorous gesticulations designed to awaken interest, especially when the large Bible was slammed shut on the sounding board of a heavily varnished deal book-rest. These sermons were referred to as 'powerful messages'.

A forty minute sermon, even with frequent sips of water from the preacher's glass, demanded stronger refreshment before the train journey home. We were not allowed to 'stay up' whilst he consumed vast quantities of bread and cheese, washed down with Guinness (known as Stout in our household, as that did not relate too obviously with the worldly advertising of a branded product). Delicious smells wafted under the dining room door and along the corridor of our bungalow to our appreciative noses, as we lay listening to the more relaxed sing-songing of his voice in social intercourse and fellowship. Twin and I agreed, with the spice of wickedness, it was the same smell we loved as it drifted from the mysterious and intriguing odours of many Ilford public houses.

Other memories of him are squeaky boots, grey spats and clanking fob-laden watch chain. He also emanated bitter rank smells we were certain came from pipe smoking (not approved by the Brethren), which we never saw him indulge, but which reminded us of the aroma surrounding the Park Keeper in South Park, Seven Kings, as he emerged in rich fog from his hut after elevenses. I sometimes wonder whether adults appreciate the acute sense of smell small children have with their unpolluted, unsophisticated and untrained noses. Going into the house we could identify any visitor by smell and enjoy the response, "How did you know it was me?"

Loxford Hall, Kingston Road, Ilford, is still there, but semi-derelict. It was owned and managed by the Exclusive Brethren or Kellyites, as sometimes called because of following the teachings of William Kelly, rather than J N Darby of the Raven Brethren, both prolific authors and expositors of Scripture. There was no cross fertilisation of doctrine between the various branches of Brethren, although they all came under the category of Fundamentalists, viewing and expounding the Bible as being literally true in every detail - for instance, Jonah really was swallowed by a great fish and vomited up alive after three days.

Brethren did not approve of an ordained, full-time ministry. The Elders of the Assemblies were known as the Oversight and they arranged services, inviting preachers for the evening Gospel Meetings and paid upkeep bills. Mature men who had shown faithfulness over many years would be invited to join the Oversight after prayerful consideration in what was known as an After Meeting following the morning service.

Loxford Hall advertised two services on their notice board - 'Lord's Day 11 am. Breaking of Bread... 6.30 pm. Gospel Meeting, ALL WELCOME'. Twin and I counted ourselves fortunate not being required to attend both. For a time there was a 2.30 p.m. Sunday School which we joined until we moved further away and could not walk home in the morning, have lunch and then walk back in time: for this we were thankful. No children, adolescents or even visitors would dream of saying, "I don't want to go to church today." Parental or host's decree was absolute!

The happiest Sunday of early childhood was when Father altered the clocks on the correct day, but in the wrong direction and we arrived at Loxford Hall as everybody was coming out. Father was so irritable on the long walk home that Twin and I had to restrain our jubilation and only give thumbs-up signs behind his bristling back. We ate Sunday lunch that day at 3.45 pm and had afternoon tea after dark.

How we both managed to sit through morning meetings beginning at 11 am and rarely finishing before 12.45, I cannot imagine. When our maternal grandmother lived in Ilford we were allowed to sit either side of her, resting heads in sleep on her life-like skunk fur. She was only too pleased to have a legitimate excuse for sitting down during hymns of interminable length and decreasing speed. We loved her dearly, but she moved back to Kent and we sat either side of our parents in future.

The hall reeked of half-burnt gas and chair bottom-warmed varnish. The only ventilation came from rectangular boxes on the walls open at the top, with metal hands pointing up for a dribble of fresh air or down for continuing fug. Varnished chairs with book slots behind were arranged in a circle round the table in the middle of the hall, the table being covered with an immaculate creakingly starched cloth, fresh every week, on which stood a decanter of red wine, a large glass tumbler and a serviette-covered plate holding a cottage loaf of white bread.

There were four rows of chairs at the back and the third row carried a well-lettered notice on sprung steel prongs facing the fourth row proclaiming, THOSE NOT IN FELLOWSHIP PLEASE SIT BEHIND THIS BOARD. Several unbaptised people, often courting the baptised, but not yet welcomed into full fellowship, or visitors from other Brethren offshoots not in group fellowship or those who had forgotten a letter of introduction or the extremely rare casual visitor... all such, sat 'behind the board'.

One thing in favour of the Brethren was that those behind the board were never proferred the offertory box; not that it would have been considered tainted, worldly money, but genuinely seen as unseemly to expect outsiders to contribute towards running expenses of the Assembly to which they did not belong.

There was no liturgy or sermon. We sat in silence until a 'brother' (never a 'sister') felt moved to announce a hymn which was sung without benefit of harmonium. In the evening Gospel Meeting the piano or harmonium was allowed, but at 11 am the boldest brother (again never a sister) would strike up the note vocally, without even the benefit of a tuning fork. Sometimes by the third line it became obvious to all concerned that the opening note had been either too low or too high and the complete tune was rapidly becoming impossible for normal human voices. With resolutely straight faces we stopped singing and an even bolder brother, possibly, but necessarily, more talented, would try an opening note at a better level. Restraining mirth required painful exacting effort in order to conquer.

Bath night amusements in the splash time before drying often included Twin starting a tune on the wrong note to see how low we could go before defeat. We never used words, as this would have been known as taking the Name of the Lord in vain: 'la, la' served our purpose very well and produced smiles from Mother in a discreet way.

At the Sunday morning meeting, before the service formally began, a letter of introduction would be read by a leading brother. "To the saints assembled at Loxford Hall - greetings in our Lord and Saviour Jesus Christ. We commend to you our beloved sister in the Lord from the Assembly gathered together in Stepney..." This explained to us why she was sitting in front of the 'board' as a full baptised member of the Plymouth Brethren. Twin and I were very proud when a similar letter was read out during the 'intimations' when we were holidaying in Southend for a long week-end - "Our beloved brother and sister, Laurence and Annie Ford, and their two **blessings...**"

Formal liturgy was anathema, but Brethren's services over the years had developed an unwritten pattern of what they called 'decent and seemly order'. After the opening hymn would be a long pause for meditation and private prayers and devotions; eyes firmly closed if not focused on the floor. Then came a throat-clearing from a brother who felt led to offer extemporary prayer in colourful pious phrases strongly influenced by Apostolic style from the Epistles in the Authorised Version of the Bible. We soon learnt, from

107

preliminary noises, which brother was to partake in worship; known bores meant eyes shut in dreams of future or past holidays; eccentrics, fond of exaggerated facial expressions, inspired slit-eyed viewing, whilst concentrating on demure facial composure.

The main emphasis during morning worship was that of thankfulness for salvation and God was therefore truly praised and exalted. We were taught that the morning meeting was a **believers'** gathering for worship, fellowship and breaking of bread in obedience to the Lord's command and therefore prayers for the world and its troubles would be out of place; such prayers, generously offered, were considered more fitting in the evening Gospel Meeting.

The congregation came from all backgrounds. In Loxford Hall we had a bank manager, school teacher, accountant, several shopkeepers, shop assistants, self employed craftsmen, unemployed artisans, unemployable misfits, the retired of all walks of life and, once, a burglar who had served his time. We liked him because he could draw anything at lightning speed and make inanimate objects smile or scowl at a stroke. As far as proselytising was concerned Brethren took no account of class. "We must win **all** for the Lord."

After another pause in the morning meeting, during which we counted ticks on the wall-clock which seemed to become louder as time lengthened, another brother would reach for his Bible with slightly exaggerated movements intended to warn and discourage any other brother similarly motivated, and would then stand up in a determined way, interpreted by other brothers as 'hold back' and then read a 'portion - laid-on-his-heart' that morning. If he was fairly young it would be regarded as unseemly if an exposition or exhortation was attempted; one of the Elders would draw him aside afterwards to explain it was not right to seek pre-eminence in expounding

Scriptures at his age.

Father was frowned upon with his rapidly increasing knowledge of Biblical languages and his occasional use of a Greek or Hebrew word in exegesis. He was considered too young and was told so. At about this time he hired a room in Ilford Town Hall and held monthly Bible classes for anybody interested; an early 'ecumenical' effort, before the word had been brought into popular use. He told Mother he was not labouring over Hebrew and Greek purely for personal enlightenment, but to use that knowledge explaining and commending God's Word to the hungry or curious.

If a Loxford Hall brother with a message 'laid on his heart' from a Bible passage was a member of the Oversight, he felt free to expound at great length and often with hair splitting exactitude explain maybe only one phrase in a particular verse. Other brethren would nod wisely, others nod off to awaken with a jerk, as they quickly attempted an expression of appreciation after such deep contemplation of the wisdom offered.

As a welcome distraction I sat opposite a friend who could be sent into helpless giggles when grimaced at; this required a certain amount of skill to escape parental detection. If body movements were avoided facial distortions could be exercised silently and with devastating effect. On one notable day he burst forth with uncontrollable laughter and was removed by his mother for audible chastisement. "Your Peter made my Alan laugh," she said irately after the service. On being questioned by Mother later I was pleasantly surprised at the lack of punishment dished out or even threatened for the future. Twin and I suspected Mother thought Alan had been making faces at me!

As the morning meeting progressed other extempore prayers were offered, readings and exhortations given and hymns draggingly sung. After maybe one hour a leading brother would rise to approach the Lord's Table with dignity to read a short portion from the Epistles concerning the Last Supper, followed by a prayer; then, solemnly lifting the loaf, he would break it open. Sometimes in humid weather the crust had become leathery and required considerable effort, but always there was the delicious smell of new bread. The plate was then passed from person to person and a small piece picked off and consumed in silence in reverent remembrance of the broken body of Christ on the Cross. Even as small children we were impressed by the obvious sincerity and depth of feeling and the round faced mahogany clock produced a louder tick in support.

When all those 'in front of the board' had partaken, the wine was poured into the tumbler with another prayer accompaniment referring to and giving thanks for the shed blood of Christ and its saving power for repentant sinners. The wine was circulated for all to sip (except us, as juniors and thus not fully authenticated). This solemn and impressive celebration of Holy Communion was the highlight of the service and performed with maximum dignity and reverence as the central, most important, part of public worship; strangely, and certainly not acknowledged as such, akin to the traditional Roman Catholic faithfulness in the observance of the Mass.

One Sunday a young man felt moved to act as President and broke the bread; he was taken aside afterwards by the Elders for a gentle, but firm, reprimand. The Oversight, he was told, would let him know when they considered him worthy enough to preside at the Breaking of Bread. He took no offence and readily recognised the traditional respect for the wisdom of age and experience.

Before the Meeting was over, one of the senior brethren would then give a 'final word', which could be up to twenty minutes in length and, as far as we could gather, never arranged or prepared beforehand, and certainly delivered without notes. There must have

110

been an unwritten pecking order, understood by the mature members, but never discussed or acknowledged openly. On the walk home, Father did occasionally mention subjects he would dearly love to expound, but Mother, being born and bred Brethren, said, "I don't think you ought to, just yet, Laurie."

On one occasion, long savoured and much mimicked by Twin and me, one brother rose to his feet to give a word at the same time as a very deaf brother also felt moved. Neither appeared to be aware of the other. Both spoke devoutly and some sleepily closed eyes opened with curiosity. Ours were wide open in eager anticipation of disaster and adult embarrassment, only to be disappointed when a conveniently placed brother to the less deaf expositor tugged his sleeve in the same way the conductor pulled the bell rope in an Ilford tram, with the same effect.

During all prayers and exhortations a talented young woman translated into deaf and dumb digital language for the benefit of a deaf mute. On rare occasions, when she was absent, a not-so-talented brother would deputise, but by his slow finger speed we all knew he was giving a very brief precis and so did the deaf mute, who, in her frustration, tapped her umbrella on the floor and made grunting noises of disapproval.

After the final prayer (never a blessing - only **God** blessed) there was often an 'after meeting' for Elders. Fortunately for us, facing a long walk home, Father was not eligible. Normally matters discussed were to do with donations from the generous collections to various widows or unfortunates, including the deaf mute.

The Assembly was entirely self supporting. Sometimes we saw the Oversight counting and apportioning the money. The collecting box with handles at both ends had a sloping slot at the top for coins and at the side a round hole through which rolled bank notes were

111

inserted. We deduced these were rolled at home and kept in waistcoat pockets, as no brother was ever seen or heard rolling one during services. Several regularly gave notes, even in the 20s. Before the Welfare State, these generous benefactions were greatly appreciated and desperately needed: a measure of the sincerity of the Brethren endeavouring to live according to their understanding of Scripture.

One colourful character, Mr Gore, with long white beard, somewhat stained around the mouth, bent back and fascinating black pin head sized holes in his cheeks (we thought they were war wounds) sat in the front row. He was very deaf and used a cupped hand as ear trumpet whilst leaning further and further forward to catch every word from a mumbling brother.

Unfortunately he had a weakness which afflicted suddenly and in the middle of a learned discourse would fumble for his two sticks to shuffle into the ante-room which sported a noisy flushing system. Some speakers charitably paused until he fumbled and puffed his way back. Woe betide us if we giggled.

Mother frequently invited him to Sunday lunch (we always said 'dinner') which was then late, because Father arm in arm with him walked home at a snail's pace. He was an accomplished pianist, highly intelligent and well educated, but clearly bereft of feminine care. He played the piano and sang in a quavering falsetto until afternoon tea, then Father walked him home before the evening Gospel Meeting. We found his eccentric looks and behaviour very entertaining. He did not appear to notice our existence!

Miss Pine, the deaf mute, also came to Sunday dinner and Twin and I learnt deaf and dumb language in order to sign "Good morning" or "Good-bye". We progressed to "This is our cat" and she was overjoyed. A pad of paper and pencils were placed on the dining room table so Mother could provide the correct food to written order. We found she was extremely quick on the uptake when asked whether she wanted more treacle pudding. For our halting efforts at finger language she patted us each under the chin and, once when we had rehearsed a long sentence about my rabbit and Twin's kittens, she kissed us both. With the cruelty of children we likened her prickly kiss to that of our animals.

One memorable day Father brought her home in a newly acquired Riley fabric saloon, when raining. As she clambered out and opened her capacious black umbrella, several apples rolled out across the pavement and rebounded from our fence into the gutter to be retrieved by us, accompanied by Father's stifled guffaws. We were rewarded by the unabashed Miss Pine with an apple each. After lunch Father signed he would drive her home.

He opened the front passenger door and she stepped on to the seat and, with dignity, composed herself on the top of the backrest! The seat cushion, a new-fangled pneumatic invention filled with air, not designed for old ladies' heels, gave way audibly under her weight, whereupon she fell slowly backwards into the rear foot-well with legs jammed against the head-lining; her head bent painfully in the back seat squab. The problem was how to get her out without damage. Finally, not helped by Father's hilarity, we opened the rear door and I eased her feet from the roof, Twin tried ineffectually to raise her bottom from the foot--well, as Father pulled her head-first on to the pavement. Luckily, she seemed to enjoy the experience and sportingly shared our mirth. When arriving at her bed-sitting room over a shop in Ilford Lane, she insisted, with urgent gesticulations, we should come upstairs to receive a toffee.

How Miss Pine would have survived the welfare starved 1920s without the loving care of the Plymouth Brethren, I tremble to think. Nowadays, of course, her lot would have greatly improved in every way. She would never be referred to as 'deaf and dumb' or 'deaf mute', but recognised as being 'deaf without speech' in the unlikely event of being unable to respond to expert modern methods of encouraging and teaching the 'profoundly deaf' to speak and overcome many of the inevitable vocal distortions of the hard of hearing.

The fact that Miss Pine made grunting noises would be regarded in this enlightened age as an opportunity to train her in audible communication. Her alertness would be noted at once and not only finger spelling, but also the beautifully expressive and graceful sign language taught, so that her possibly distorted English could be supported with signs in either of two visual methods.

Full marks to the Plymouth Brethren for their efforts in 1928!

*Father 4th from right in back row, after discharge from Birmingham gaol as a "conchie": then in Non-Combatant Corps, stationed at Tilbury. Front row: the Collins family − Mother 2nd from left*

# PREACHERS

Most preachers came from other Brethren's Meetings in Essex, occasionally imports were welcomed from Kent or Sussex and, once or twice, well-known Brethren from London. Several were colourful characters.

One such was known as an expert on Palestine and during his sermon would don authentic Eastern garments to add dramatic effect as background to visual aids on a blackboard. He toured the country, exercising his speciality and, because so reputed for his knowledge of the Holy Land, he was offered and accepted an important, well-paid position in America under the auspices of one of their numerous Bible-Belt religious groups. He was given a well-publicised doctorate, ensuring him a lucrative retirement in his homeland. A few years later, when Twin and I fully understood adult conversations with whispered innuendoes wafting our way, we learnt he had never set foot in Palestine.

A preacher we always endeavoured to hear was a 'born again' weightlifter with a rumoured 56 inch chest and even bigger waist, which had to be eased up the pulpit steps with vigorous exhalations, every breath adding to the general excitement and anticipation. He never failed to mention in his pre-ambles how he lifted a live donkey at country fairs, until the Lord lifted him from a worldly life. We enjoyed relating to his sermons which were referred to as 'home-spun' with language rich in illustrations and anecdotes. To us he was 'the tops' and we believed (quite rightly, I'm sure) every word he said. We thought it a lovely, slightly wicked glimpse into the world beyond our Plymouth Brethren shelter. We noticed with joy how each illustration gained over the years in gesticulation, but, unlike so many other preachers under whom we suffered, were without factual embellishments. As devotees of his sermons we were, I suppose, in a juvenile context, experts! Certainly ardent fans, at least.

We were sufficiently experienced in sermon contents, as delivered in our narrow circle, to recognise exaggerations and accretions if they developed, particularly from those who had, in their own words, been 'delivered from worldliness' and all too often continued preaching about only **one** significant event in their lives, without attempting to develop or even suggest any possible progress in the life of Faith.

As the preachers were never professionals, any idiosyncrasies tended to blossom rather than shrivel as they might have done under the discipline of academic training. Nevertheless, there was no lack of sincerity and enthusiasm - and they certainly knew their Bibles.

Twin and I could never understand why the wife and family of one leading brother allowed him to add 'er, er,' at the end of every phrase without protest. "Dearly beloved, er, er, we welcome, er, er, our brother, er, er, from, er, er, Walthamstow Assembly, er, er, as our preacher, er, er, tonight. He has come, er, er, a long way in such, er, er, inclement weather, er, er, and we look forward, er, er, to his message, er, er, er, er, tonight." This style was devastatingly easy to mimic, providing family or Assembly Elders were not within earshot.

Tolerance was another plus mark for Plymouth Brethren, who, if questioned, would have said, "The Lord gave him an impediment in his speech, who are we to criticise? Praise God for his **talents,** in charity and forbearance, brother."

There were many visiting preachers with ponderous methods of oration with remarkably little humour. Whenever we listened attentively, which was rare, the effect was invariably depressing. Rigid formulae were used to convict hearers of sin, even though most, if not all, were full and active members of the Gospel Hall. Then followed an enlarging of the perils of eternal punishment, this led to repentance and forgiveness; anybody sufficiently convicted could be counselled and 'led to Christ' at the end of the service. The conclusion of the Gospel talk was 'the appeal' and woe betide any visiting brother who failed to make it powerful.

The Elders realised this type of message was likely to be most productive preached to non-believers and wisely, so they thought, initiated open-air meetings in Ilford Lane three quarters of an hour before the Sunday evening Gospel Meeting. A portable harmonium was manhandled to the pavement and hymn books distributed to all supporters; one or two brave brethren hovered on the edge of the circle acting as pious barkers to challenge passers-by to come and join the singing. If they responded, perhaps they would like to come round the corner to the Hall and hear the Gospel message starting shortly. In theory a good idea; in practice a good method of packing pavements on the other side of the road.

Feeling desperately self-conscious and with ears attuned to fruity comments coming across the road, we cringed in the circle of singers. Only once can I recall anybody coming in from the road to the Gospel Meeting and he left halfway through, when the preacher's thumping fist on the pulpit galvanised him into making an unsteady, beer-fumed exit.

The Elders often experienced difficulty in providing preachers every Sunday; when desperate, they asked our favourite, a small man with a squeaky, one-note voice. His speciality, and indeed only subject, was the Old Testament Tabernacle and detailed instructions for its construction and use were passed on to us, as given by God to Moses and recorded at length in the Book of Exodus. It was not his subject matter which captivated us, so much as his appearance, mannerisms and visual aids. He arrived at the Gospel Hall on a specially adapted Rudge Whitworth bicycle with chain enclosed in an oil bath. A well made extended wooden carrier over the rear wheel was covered with oilcloth (as used on kitchen tables) and under this was strapped his home-made model of the Tabernacle. Under the crossbar were slung rolled up pictures of his subject with arrows pointing from various features to notes in the margin. Over the front of the pulpit he hung a half-size coloured picture of the High Priest, heavily varnished to prolong life, and steadily darkening every year. The handlebars supported an adapted metal container, similar to an errand boy's delivery bicycle; crammed into this were neatly boxed models and smaller varnished pictures of priests' garments, golden candlesticks, brazen altars and many other illustrations, which he rarely had time to use, except at Conferences lasting all day, to which we never went, but heard about by keeping quiet whilst parents talked over our heads.

The leading Elder on Tabernacle-talk night hovered in the vestibule to announce, "He's here!", whereupon younger brethren hastened to help the preacher, bicycle and accoutrements into the cloak-room. Boxes, banners, folding easels and displays were carried in solemn procession to the pulpit, the harmonium providing background music from *Sankey's Sacred Songs and Solos*. We waited in joyous anticipation for the entrance of the **specialist** complete with round edged stiff white collar, protruding starched shirt cuffs and slightly too big shirt-dickey flapping against his waist as he walked. It was the legs we savoured, in fawn breeches and

118

brilliantly polished leather gaiters, extending from just below the knee to ankle and overlapping brown squeaky boots reflecting gas light in mirror finish.

Marching determinedly to the pulpit he was followed by faint smells of oil, carbolic soap, maturing varnish, boot polish and what we later learnt was snuff. Occasionally the Elder delegated to assist with props was negligent and, to our delight, the footstool behind the pulpit for the benefit of short preachers was missing and our favourite began to pray after the opening hymn with only forehead visible. Mr Er, er, generally seemed to be the Elder responsible and, after a shove from his lanky daughter, moved various pieces of furniture so that the preacher's complete face could eventually be seen after stepped stages from one kneeler to another was placed until a final plank from the back of the harmonium spanned the gap between two piles of rustled-up props. Twin and I hoped his enthusiasm would lead to a step backwards and total disaster; invariably it led instead to a longer period of high-pitched droning with cane pointer shakily indicating features of the visual aids. In winter, the combination of gas fires and breath resulted in condensation pouring off the varnished pictures to become stagnant pools on the scrubbed deal floorboards, to us a constant source of speculation as to how far the ragged edged stain could spread before the meeting ended. Soporific indulgence from the adult congregation was alleviated by a generally invigorating closing hymn.

Once we were honoured by being allowed to light the wick of his paraffin-fuelled bull's-eye bicycle lamp. With shining leather gaiters and whiffs of paraffin he pedalled away for another preaching engagement.

Such eccentric characters seem to have faded from the scene, which may be as well as doubtless

119

they would be ridiculed and any tolerance shown to them might be in order to exploit entertainment value. At least our favourite preacher promoted sober instruction to be given later by the Elders on the symbolism of the Tabernacle at subsequent week-night home-based Bible readings; he was also respected for self-taught knowledge, enthusiasm and his non-stipendary ministry. One wonders how far he would progress today without even the most modest diploma in Religious Knowledge.

England seemed to be more Christianity-minded between the two wars and open air meetings with soap box and harmonium on the pavement were tolerated as normal Sunday evening events in the larger suburbs, possibly even extended charitably to the occasional Saturday afternoon, as well.

Two episodes still haunt me and promote a nervous goose-flesh feeling. Near Ilford Station was a cul-de-sac leading to an arcade, adjacent to Bodger's Store. With no through traffic it was an ideal site for hucksters, quacks and evangelists. A middle-aged man and a young woman were standing on a crude soap box platform raised two feet above street level. The front carried a banner neatly, but inexpertly, lettered 'God is love'. The man was explaining that the young lady had recently become a Christian and had given her life to God and would now give her testimony to that wonderful fact. The pale-faced young woman now began to talk about her conversion and how a similar experience could be enjoyed by everyone listening. If they felt moved by the Spirit of God they were welcome to accept a form from the minister as he walked through the crowd, to fill in details of name and address and be put in touch with the nearest Gospel Hall (Billy Graham did not invent this approach), all free of charge, as the Gospel of Salvation was free. A genuine feeling of the sincerity of the message

120

pervaded the crowd and overcame the bustling noises of Ilford Broadway. Some people appeared thoughtful and there was no barracking as the girl was wholesome and obviously genuine in her convictions. Then a navy-blue serge suited man pushed his way from the back of the crowd, shouting obscenities, and spat in the face of the girl with a venomous forward jerk of his head. For a moment motionless, as spittle slid across her cheek, she then burst into tears. The minister leapt to the platform and announced a hymn, the harmonium wheezed into action, as the Broadway flower seller elbowed her way forward to proffer a snuff-stained handkerchief, "Here y'are, duckie, better luck next time." Mother propelled us back to Sandyhill Road in silence; after such a display of hatred, thoughts precluded chatter.

The other episode was in a hamlet near Abridge. Essex was still very rural around Hainault, Chigwell Row, Theydon Bois and Lambourne End and cycling much safer with sparse motor traffic. Young people in our circle were poor and bus fares were considered a waste of money if pedal-power was available. A keen group of youngsters from the Gospel Hall decided to take the Good News to the villages; they asked the senior Sunday School and Youth Group members for support, if they had bicycles. Having just acquired my first bicycle for six shillings and sixpence [$32\frac{1}{2}$p], which was already a creaky antique, I volunteered to join the group. We set off. In nervous anticipation, chatter and banter decreased in proportion to knowledge of what lay ahead. As far as I was concerned this was double. My chain was strained to breaking point and I only had vaguely reported ideas of what was to come. Broken chains could be mended, I hoped, but broken or inadequate 'messages' perhaps not!

We reached the selected hamlet that Sunday

afternoon and laid the cycles to rest in a circle on the small green. We formed a separate, very self-conscious circle around them and were exhorted by the leader to bow our heads in prayer. He beseeched the Almighty to give us courage and guidance in spreading the Gospel. In my case, to no effect.

By this time several net curtains fluttered to give views of this strange invasion. One of our bolder spirits opened the enterprise by shouting, "This is a faithful saying, and worthy of all acceptance, that Christ Jesus came into the world to save sinners." This was followed with other texts shouted by each member in turn; some with high--pitched voices through nerves, others husky and strained from years of talking against machinery noises in Bow and Stratford and, finally, weak teen-age voices in various stages of breaking. In a long pause, I realised I was expected to contribute. Acute embarrassment and lack of a retentive memory for texts rendered me dumb and flushed.

Net curtains fell into place with alacrity and several gardeners melted away when the nature of the gathering became apparent; an uncanny stillness descended on the hamlet. After several additional rounds of shouted texts, the first verse of a Sankey hymn was sung from memory and the leader prayed that God's Word would speak to any needy soul. Then we cycled home, in my case with intense relief. Worthy as the motive was, I felt it was a pathetic and misplaced evangelical effort, probably of more spiritual benefit to the donors than recipients.

It was a long and silent slog home, on my part from guilt at cowardice and wobbly faith and shame at a secret resolve never to go on another cycle mission. The other members, I guessed, were nervously exhausted and possibly wrestling with doubts as to efficacy and the propriety of shouting unexplained, out-of-context texts, without some

122

sort of academic training or direction.

Professional missions and gatherings, of which there were many, were a very different matter and, because attendance required travelling by bus, train or tram, were great treats. 'Tea Meetings' were our favourite and held on Saturday afternoons from 2 to 5 pm. Several erudite brethren would lecture on specific and previously well-advertised books in the Bible, with periodical discussions generously open to all. This was above our heads in content, but of great interest concerning mannerisms and unusual accents and in guessing how well or badly some brethren controlled irritability under verbal or nit-picking challenge.

An hour would pass until two Sisters rose quietly to slip out of a side door behind the pulpit to organise tea. Shortly, the sour smell of inefficiently burnt gas from the ring under a battered tea-urn pervaded the gathering, encouraging us that tea was on the way. Unlike today, gas burners were large cast-iron affairs resembling octopus tentacles trained and fixed into a circle; they were also difficult to wash free of spilt and burnt fat and, if removed, awkward to reposition. Not surprisingly, they were generally left alone and any spillage burnt into irremovable black deposits. Gas and air holes became obstructed and any still operative, if under full gas pressure, were soon overloaded and unable to cope with the flow or provide odour-free combustion. Gradually the smell increased and steam condensed on windows and gloss painted walls, the clattering of crockery intruded into learned discourses; Twin and I revived in anticipation of sickly cream cakes.

The leading Brother, in response to unseen signs we never detected, fumbled his watch from fob pocket, flicked open the hunter lid and announced with due dignity and subdued enthusiasm that we

123

were now to 'partake of refreshments provided by our beloved Sisters'. This was the time for which we had suffered and had already decided in private signals how many cream cakes we would try to extract.

Bakers' trays of meat and fish paste sandwiches were circulated by volunteer Sisters. The bread was pappy, white tin loaf in square section, such as we never had at home and therefore much more interesting. In the days when it was normal for children to be told to eat several slices of bread and butter before moving on to cakes and buns, it was exhilarating actually to begin with paste sandwiches.

On the table normally used for 'Breaking of Bread' were trays of white and pink iced cakes, macaroons and marzipan-edged window cakes. Elderly Sisters indulged the Twins, as we ate huge quantities of such alien delights denied our frugal everyday menu. Mother pretended not to notice.

If we were lucky, left-overs were bagged up and distributed to families with children or to widows or anybody finding it hard to make ends meet. These Tea Meetings were free of charge, but the Brethren, after a huddle in the corner, gave the Sisters a major contribution towards costs. In our overheard 'under the door' conversations we never heard a grumble from our parents when discussing Tea Meetings and Father's financial contribution.

Larger Conventions in the Memorial Hall, Farringdon Street, London EC4, were paid for by free-will offerings held during procedures. The lecturers were not paid, but travelling expenses offered and sometimes accepted. Many leading brethren were self-made men of substance even in those days of slump and gloomy self-destroying unemployment.

The Victorian and Christian ethic of hard work

and honest dealing was still operative between the wars; most Brethren prospered as these qualities were recognised and admired by the general public. We enjoyed these rare trips to London and if we had been good were taken to a Lyons' Tea Shop for fish and chips served by black and white uniformed Nippies; females of various ages united in looking worn out and hot. Air conditioning was primitive and the atmosphere thick with tobacco smoke and frying fumes.

Domestically frying was always done with lard or home-made dripping, smells familiar to us all, but ABC and Lyons' Tea Shops obviously used sharp--smelling commercial oils or fats unobtainable at home. Twin and 1 loved these odoriferous marks of rare treats, having become immune to the clinging smells of home frying we and all our friends had on our clothes.

Mission services in the largest halls available were well attended to hear preachers as famous in their day as Billy Graham post-war. Our parents rarely attended, but allowed us to be taken by keen friends. Preaching techniques were similar to many modern methods. Hearty singing, short prayers and readings gradually produced a receptive atmosphere for the great man himself to preach, maybe for forty to forty-five minutes. Towards the close of the Gospel Message repentant sinners were urged to come forward for Christ; this required skilful manipulation of the mood of all present and precise timing in order to be effective, as a suitable hymn was announced to be sung with heads bowed. Between verses, the preacher would ask those who had made a decision to raise a hand... then... "Praise God, and bless you both". This would continue until he felt led to conclude by inviting those who had indicated surrender to come forward for counselling. Twin and 1 would, with bowed heads, peep at the steady stream of supplicants filling the aisles. Frequently we felt guilty at not responding every time ourselves.

Some Missions appeared non-productive and we felt sorry for the preacher who covered his desperation by prolonging the last hymn with frequent verses repeated... "This may well be your only chance... don't delay... come forward NOW... as we sing the verse again, come forward to the glory of God!"

The long silence between penultimate and last verse was agonizing and we often confided to each other later on in bed that we could easily have 'decided' dozens of times from charitable motives.

Many rich phrases were used in the evangelical approach to ministry. One, typical of the time, came from a Welsh evangelist who, towards the end of his sermon, referred to the terrors of Hell for those rejecting the Gospel, by bellowing in a melodious 'Valley' accent, "The caverns of Hell will echo with the cries of the damned - will **you** be there?"

Radio, or wireless as it was then called, was in its infancy and television only just emerging as a future possibility, fulfilling predictions in sceptically received science fiction. The spoken word 'live' thus had far more effect, especially if projected by preachers who had grasped the importance of reaching the back rows of vast halls without the benefit of microphones. One famous preacher, Dinsdale Young, could fill the huge and packed Westminster Central Hall with the sound of his voice without visible effort or amplification. Voice projection was a vital part of the successful preacher's repertoire.

Viable hearing aids had not arrived; when they did, in the mid-30s, they were cumbersome box camera sized contraptions carried on handles. One old lady we knew used a copper ear trumpet which she pointed in the direction of the speaker. In social gatherings she would advance towards her selected target using the trumpet as a churchwarden's stave; dipping to mouth level she would say, grandly, "There's no need to shout." If the conversation proved to be boring, or otherwise not to her liking, she would withdraw the trumpet with devastating effect upon morale. Having to enunciate carefully into the wide end of an ear trumpet is a powerful incentive to economise on words. That particular old lady, intelligent, well educated and running a highly successful second-hand bookshop probably valued her deafness as an invaluable weapon against boredom.

*Top deck, Tilbury–Gravesend ferry, Spring, 1931*

# TRAVEL

Travel in the 20s, as far as we were concerned, was mainly carried out on foot. Children in our neighbourhood walked anything up to three miles to school without escorts. The modern scene of many parent-driven automobiles queuing outside schools to take children home would have been unthinkable and, indeed, viewed as 'spoiling' the child.

Main streets and suburban residential avenues were, of course, far safer then than now. We were, naturally, well taught as to the importance of never receiving sweets or heeding messages from complete strangers. Twin and I, each walking several miles every day, never experienced any challenge of worrying proportions or ominous content or portent.

One unsolicited, fortuitous gift enjoyed was a stump of soggy Manikin cigar discarded whilst still burning. When the discarder disappeared into busy Longbridge Road, we rescued the smoking remnant from the hedge and sucked a few bubbly whiffs with great aplomb. The after-taste proved unexpectedly powerful and Twin suggested breath fumes might be inexplicably strong and definitely incriminating in our nicotine-free home; so we chewed chrysanthemum leaves before going home.

Public transport reeked of tobacco and Father, a life-long non-smoker arrived home with every article of clothing impregnated and even his kiss carried nicotine on moustache hairs. Smoking smells were part of everyday experience and nearly everybody's habit. We were the exception.

Even on railways non-smoking provision was scarce. L.N.E.R. suburban trains catered for first, second and third class passengers. First class carriages were richly upholstered with anti-macassars, head rests and folding arms. Second class, normally for season ticket commuting people, enjoyed cloth upholstery and enclosed compartments capable of accommodating six passengers each side. Third class sat on shiny rexine seats with back-rests opening above head level, so that standing passengers could see through several compartments.

In all third class carriages smoking was allowed and only first and second class included some 'No Smoking' or 'Ladies Only' signs. Each window, in all classes, had spring loaded roller sunshades, capable of being fixed at any level in notches provided. Door windows were adjusted by hide straps reminiscent of cut-throat razor strops. Many were missing and we gathered from adult 'tut, tuts' had been sliced off for home use. Twin and I checked Father's strop and noted that it was far thinner than those on the L.M.S. line to Tilbury!

Each carriage was cleaned before every journey and all rubbish removed, apart from the cigarette cards then garnered by collectors. Smoking was popular and almost endemic and therefore a rich gathering ground for those hooked on various series of this or that portrayed in colour on the cards.

L.N.E.R. cork linoleum floors were regularly mopped and windows washed with soft bristled long--handled brooms, removing a modicum of sooty deposits. Smells of oil, steam, coal, smoke, tobacco and dusty upholstery contributed to the thrill of rare train trips.

The Barking to Tilbury line seemed more run down than the Ilford to Liverpool Street and Mother always instructed us NOT to lean our heads on the back-rest. We gathered, from overheard conversations, this was to avoid catching head lice.

Several businessmen of our acquaintance, who commuted daily, set their watches by the 8.15 am train. Engine drivers were regarded as the elite of the L.N.E.R. and many railway buffs would wait on a crowded platform saying, "It must be Fred Young," or "Maybe it's George Dawson today", as they checked watches to the sound of brakes applied either a few yards before or after the normal mark on the platform. Engine drivers understood the hero worship of children and occasionally allowed peeps into the inferno of the cabin.

Guards were important personages in impressive uniforms, complete with whistle, flag and large turnip watch in constant use. Porters swept platforms every morning, keeping an eye open for passengers with heavy luggage. They always shouted the name of the station as the train stopped and also added, for good measure, the list of subsequent stops. There was a pride apparent in belonging to the L.N.E.R., transmitting itself to passengers on waves of courtesy and general helpfulness.

To use a modern term, 'job satisfaction' was high and the customer benefited. Rewards, scarce in those days, were pensions proudly received and richly deserved after lifelong faithful service.

Trams on rails set in granite blocks extended from Chadwell Heath to Barking via Ilford Broadway. When first opened in 1903 there were $5\frac{1}{2}$ miles of tramlines from Chadwell Heath to Barkingside. The tram driver stood all the time and without weather protection. Wearing heavy leather pugs he manipulated a horizontal brass wheel with a vertical handle to regulate speed. Foul weather goggles and ankle length rubberised trench coat completed the protective clothing. A brake lever to the left was firmly clutched whilst moving; should pedestrians, dogs or vehicles appear near tramlines the driver stamped on a two inch diameter brass knob on the floor to activate a warning bell of penetrating tone.

For interior use a bell at driver's head height was worked by the conductor from a suspended cord running the length of the tram. One ring for 'stop', two for 'start' and three for 'don't stop - full up - nobody alighting'. Woe betide any child attempting to usurp such powers of command by fiddling with the bell-pull!

The economical design downstairs had seats facing the middle; underneath one row was a box of sand for temporarily covering vomit until the tram shed cleansing department was reached. Swaying motions were often quite alarming and much worse 'outside' (the term still used for 'upstairs' as a relic of the open topped horsedrawn trams before top decks were roofed) and responsible for sea-sickness symptoms and consequent results.

Smoking, only permitted upstairs, seemed to consist of strong shag roll-ups (we liked the aromatic and, to us, alien smell) or ready made Wild Woodbines (five for tuppence) in open-top paper packets.

Other practical economies included hinged seats upstairs, easily reversed for return journeys and roofed, but windowless compartments at each end for those hoping that fresh air cured nausea. If this failed, it was convenient to be ill over the brass rail, providing there was no prevailing wind. Mother graphically demonstrated one day, as the conductor encouraged her with, "Come on, missus, get it all up! THAT'S BETTER, there, there!". Twin and I warmed to his fatherly tone and were surprised that Mother seemed annoyed at such familiarity and kindness.

Both ends of the tram were identical, thus obviating turntables at termini. The driver simply opened his sliding door and walked to the other end, whilst the conductor, with long bamboo pole, hooked the overhead pick-up from one wire to the other and then, with obvious satisfaction, slid the pole into a rack beneath the tram.

131

Once at Chadwell Heath the pick-up slipped and, being spring-loaded, jerked skywards beside the feeder wires. Great consternation ensued and plentiful advice was offered by onlookers, but not taken by the experienced crew who quickly, with practised skill, restored further mobility. Meanwhile, the staff at the Terminus Café prepared tea for conductor and driver, to be poured into a white enamelled jug with chipped lid. This was lodged in the conductor's cubby hole and, with its base wider than the top, survived the hazards of lurching travel.

Were trade quiet the conductor counted coppers into paper bags and stored them beside the tea jug. We admired the slick method employed and envied the privilege of handling such wealth. I cannot remember a ten shilling note ever being offered for fare, let alone a pound note, but sometimes silver would be, and was then carefully placed in the space nearest the conductor's body in the double pocketed portable hide-till measuring approximately eight by twelve inches and worn at waist level. A nickel plated punch was slung from his other shoulder and colourful tram tickets punched and skilfully marked with round holes corresponding to fare stages, after which extra money would be needed.

Originally variously coloured tickets in wads were held in a trap with individual springs, reminiscent of mouse trap springs, the conductor carried this contraption around his neck on another strap. Much later on tickets were in perforated rolls and more convenient, especially in rush hours. As a mark of authority and satisfactory confirmation of the contract to travel, a bell rang as the punch lever was depressed.

With what would be considered then a useful amount of money in coins about his person, we never heard or contemplated the possibility of anybody

*Cranbrook Road, looking towards the park as the cricket field empties, 1936*

*Ilford tram at Chadwell Heath in 1903*

*(Photographs by courtesy of Local History Library, Redbridge)*

mugging a tram or bus conductor for his takings.

We, together with several friends, collected bus and tram tickets (train tickets had to be handed to ticket collectors at even the remotest railway stations) and these we swopped at school. Each tram or bus company had their name printed on the ticket and holiday time provided rich pickings for rarities. Children-tolerant conductors allowed us to lucky-dip in the used ticket boxes before alighting. Aunts and uncles living far away were beseeched to send local tickets in their next letter.

When trolley buses arrived in the mid-30s a clever cast aluminium gadget housing reels of thin paper was introduced. The conductor dialled a number as if telephoning and, by turning a handle, produced a printed receipt which most children considered unworthy of collecting. We changed to cigarette cards instead.

There was a certain camaraderie, especially on the lower deck of trams. On one occasion of cherished memory, a distracted mother hauled her small son on board with a chamber pot jammed over his head. After concerned discussion with the conductor whether it should be hospital, doctor's surgery or fire station, it was decided the doctor's was the nearest, meanwhile several motherly bodies tried to remove the chamber and various instructions were given as to the angle of the neck and head needed for painless removal. Muffled slobbering noises filtered out from beneath the china from time to time until the conductor pulled the bell-rope for an unscheduled stop near the doctor's road.

"You'll soon be free, sonny-boy," he said encouragingly as the tram ground to a halt, where-upon the boy gingerly lifted the chamber pot off his head and calmly handed it to his mother. The lower deck's laughter fuelled the parent's fury as she belaboured him with a shopping bag too small to contain the empty chamber. They probably walked home, as pennies were scarce and not to be wasted.

Tramlines were shallow and it worried Twin and me how lurching double-deckers remained in them. Trams were derailed, but so rarely that it made the local headlines.

Trams swayed, creaked and screeched alarmingly, but petrol driven buses added vibrations from engine pulsations and because of solid rubber tyres bumping on granite setts. Bus drivers had no glass windscreens and, in driving rain, erected canvas covers supposed to deflect rain, sleet or snow from body, thighs and legs; actually they collected water in puddles to spew on to the lap at corners.

Originally top decks were unroofed with individual canvas lap covers for inclement weather; later on roofs were added, but, strangely, the spiral staircases were left open to the elements. Temptingly smooth brass hand rails were provided for safety and, if the conductor was busy, invited rapid slides to pavement level. Hooters were externally mounted horns with deep, rather rude, voices, activated when the rubber globes were squeezed; gentle and slow gave a deep cow-like moan, quick jerks a slightly higher truncated belching sound. Twin and I, in common with most children, found parked vehicles irresistible for daring experimentation in bulbous horn blowing.

Gear boxes had no synchromesh and required double de-clutching at every gear change between scheduled stops during a very long day; hard work indeed, needing two activations of the heavy clutch pedal and considerable sensitivity to the revolutions of the engine. Lifting off the accelerator for changing up or pressing down for changing down was vital for a quiet change of gear. The absence of gear crashing noises was a tribute to the driving skills of hardy men facing all weathers without windscreens or high, free revving engines, complete with synchromesh gear boxes or, as now, automatic gear changes.

From time to time in hot weather and with a loaded bus on even an almost imperceptible incline, like that near Chigwell, we grunted to a halt and the conductor had to knock at the nearest front door to beg jugs of water for the steaming radiator. Twin and I enjoyed the wait, anticipating clouds of steam escaping from the gingerly opened radiator cap in those days embossed with the maker's name.

Motorised travel was always adventurous and arrival at any destination of more than twenty miles a subject of congratulation to driver and, if from personal experience of the car, involved an opportunity to extol its praises. Later on, hopes were expressed for a straightforward, uneventful return journey. Not by any means, from the cars Father drove, assured!

Charabancs were popular for works or church outings; they were large open-topped coaches originally solid tyred, but, by the late 20s, pneumatic tubed and tyred and therefore slightly more comfortable. Maximum speeds of 30 m.p.h. meant wind speeds were relatively unimportant unless head-on and, of course, hazardous if following. Slightly down-hill with strong following breezes was exhilarating, even if highly dangerous. Sidescreens had not yet arrived for popular use -although available on Austin Sevens from about 1923. Passengers on one side of the charabanc kept dry on the road to Southend and, unless the wind changed, got wet on the return journey. Many friendships were lost as sides were changed before returning.

Enclosed coaches arrived in the 1930s, but

excursions were still referred to as charabanc trips even after World War Two. In fact, in 1972 in Keighley, we watched an elderly lady in the bus station question the bus inspector by saying, "Are t'Blackpool charas in yet?" Without showing surprise at this fifty year leap backwards he replied, "Nay, luv, I'll let thee know."

The eastern suburbs of London were built for people who worked in the great metropolis and the L.N.E.R. conveyed them. Even in those days carriages at peak times were grossly overcrowded, thus stimulating private enterprise to attempt improvements. With the advantage of a virtually straight road (thanks to the Romans) from Colchester to Aldgate and only Brook Street Hill at Brentwood providing any form of hindrance it occurred to Edward Hillman (later to open Maylands Airport, Harold Wood) to provide a fast coach service to London under the banner of Hillman Coaches in royal blue livery. Drivers and conductors were young and slightly raffish. The main aim was to get to London before the competition; this aim, success at all costs, resulted in a popular renaming as Killman Coaches.

An indulgent relative treated Twin and me to a trip. It was as thrilling as a switchback ride in the Tivoli Gardens, Copenhagen. Fumes and heat from the overstressed engine filled the cabin and violent swerving to overtake trams on either side, with an occasional savage braking, meant the sudden illness factor was high. In bad cases of sickness, the coconut matting was neatly turned upside down until the depot cleaners could attempt, not always successfully, to improve matters.

The enterprise failed, mainly because one never knew whether the scheduled coach would arrive full or not.

Some of our younger acquaintances, making

a career in the City (today they would be called yuppies) used Hillman's and were thought rather dashing by older friends reluctant to lose the uncomfortable, but reliable London & North Eastern Railway method of arriving on time.

Twin and I speculated on the fate of one bowler hatted junior executive waiting for a coach who, seeing the approaching cloud of dust and exhaust fumes travelling at a speed to prevent the usual stop, leapt into the road waving his *Times* with one hand and elevating a despatch case as earnest of his importance, only to receive a deprecatory shrug from the conductor jammed between standing passengers. In our innocence we decided his urgent mouthing on the way to the station was a prayer that the 8.15 commuter train would be late.

Taxis evolved from Hansom cabs (hence the term 'cabbie') to petrol driven vehicles with spacious interiors upholstered in hide and snugly enclosed, with windows and a glass division isolating customer from cabbie, who made do in the front with no side protection apart from the height of the luggage on the platform to his left, where a private car passenger seat would have been sited. A good example of how designers can be so influenced by the past that they shy away from original thinking; after all, stage coach drivers, brougham and carriage drivers all lacked protection, so did the early lorry and bus drivers and even chauffeurs in large limousines: who would dare break such a tradition?

Between the wars wool was a much more important ingredient in clothing, and the cab driver thus better protected against hard weather. Long-johns in thick, so-called lambs' wool, and slightly thinner vests with long sleeves in cream, aging to cheddar cheese colour, less prickly wool, no doubt helped his survival in adverse conditions. Maybe the slightly abrasive sardonic wit of present-day London taxi drivers was born in those days of class consciousness and draughty gulfs between servant and master.

Twin and I never experienced a taxi ride. My only opportunity, offered by a wealthy relative, was aborted by my screams of horror at clattering engine noises filling the darkened interior: a rather irritable tram ride followed. No further offers of prestigious travel were made because of the 'difficult' twins; tough on my sister who only sucked her thumb during my exhibition of taxi-phobia.

Taxi cabs were generally of the cabriolet type with passenger compartment covered by an opening leather hood supported by nickel-plated hood irons, as favoured on the perambulators of the day. In the early 30s chromium plate took over as it required less maintenance for a high gloss. In slack moments cabbies could be seen wax-proofing the leather.

One well known Bedfordshire taxi owner, even in the late 40s, still used a huge, immediately post- -Great War Wolseley hire car with two steps each side for mounting into the cab. There was no self-- starter; on receiving instructions the owner/driver flourished a starting handle from under his seat and lurched towards the bonnet, his artificial leg swinging sideways and, at the moment of handle entry, sticking out backwards as he expertly yanked upwards, lovingly adding a flourish, never failing to fire the engine into leisurely, reliable throbs. Many locals spurned modern taxis on offer, preferring a time honoured alternative.

Every spring, between trips, the owner rubbed down the panels with water and holystone, in order to repaint with ordinary gloss paint: he did this whilst on the taxi rank. Years later, on a trip to Bedford, we saw that same handsome conveyance parked and polished outside his retirement home.

Memories of horse drawn outings are rather dim. Our maternal grandfather would sometimes hire a two horse carriage to convey the family to a famous watercress farm (now long gone because of a drastically reduced water table) for afternoon tea, followed by bunches of watercress, picked while we waited. We then toured the lanes until time was up. The gentle plod, plod and occasional snorts from tossed heads, as tails swirled away troublesome flies, against the background of subdued creaking from carriage springs are sounds that live forever in nostalgic memory.

A more frequent experience of horse-drawn travel was when we were allowed to ride the shire horses back to the stables after a long day of ploughing. With our bare legs rubbing on salty sweat, we soon became sore, but Aunty Margaret, who was childless, but loved and understood children and whom we adored, would bathe our reddened limbs and apply cold cream. "You'll be alright by tomorrow," she would say, and we always were.

The tremendous power of the shire horse, truly a gentle giant, can best be felt astride the enormous back. Uncle's horses were always gentle and tolerant, perhaps they appreciated the titbits we proferred and the many evenings we sat in the stable talking to them quietly. My favourite, the biggest, was called, pertinently, 'Duke': he condescended to lower his aristocratic head to my level as we exchanged breath. Sometimes his velvety lips caressed my probably long unwashed forehead: I hope it wasn't just for the salt!

Another thrilling, but mechanical, method of travel was experienced on the Tilbury/Gravesend ferry, run by the London, Midland & Scottish Railway Company. Their wonderful craft were operated in two ways; a passenger-only service from Tilbury to Gravesend Town Pier and a car ferry service from a different landing stage in Tilbury to West Street Pier. Tilbury Docks and Landing stage were hives of activity. P & O liners with three different ethnic groups from India, mostly Goanese catering staff, Afghan engine room crew and diminutive Lascars as deck hands, poured over to Gravesend on spending sprees; all this made ferry trips more exotic.

Passenger ferries had accommodation (very temporary, of course) on two levels, the enclosed salon and the open upper deck, favoured by us. Car ferries needing more deck space offered a top deck for passengers not wishing to remain inside their cars. Both designs had engine rooms with open gratings belching gusts of warm air, thick with smells of hot oil, steam and coal. To us, peering down, it seemed like the inferno of Hell, with the addition of huge reciprocating cranks, pistons, hissing valves and varying thuds in response to alarmingly sudden clangs of a bell signalling instructions from the bridge. Fierce currents, strong winds and fast-flowing tides required great skill from skipper and crew in manoeuvring these slightly underpowered ferries alongside smoothly; many signals were given by the skipper, and to us, in our ignorance, sounded like panic when the bows bumped discreetly against the Town Pier fenders. Uncle told us later that we had indulged our imaginations, those final clangs after contact meant, "Close down for a cup of tea; next ferry in thirty minutes."

The heat below decks was intense and both stoker and engineer were permanently shiny with sweat. We thought they wore dish-cloths, until Grandma informed us they were known as 'sweat-rags' and Grandpa sold them in his shop. Twin and I discussed whether people wore such things in Hell, where surely the heat must be even worse than in ferry engine rooms. We enquired of Grandma, who replied, "I hope you'll never find out!"

# MOTOR CARS

In our income bracket motor car ownership was rare, partly because of cost and the uncertainty of steady employment, but also because public transport in the suburbs was plentiful and relatively cheap. Cars dropped their value very rapidly and there was no such thing as a 'collector's car'.

Father, having done rather well with his advertising enterprise as his secondary occupation, decided a car would be useful for outings and also for visiting clients in the evening or at weekends. He noticed a 1928 Riley 9 fabric saloon (the Monaco) at Smith Motors in Goodmayes; considered a very sporty car, the Riley Nine depreciated at a higher rate than more sedate family cars, the reason being that people surmised the engine may have been thrashed. This proved to be true with the car Father bought.

Driving tests had not been thought of and driving instructors were any friends or relatives who could be persuaded to oblige for an hour or two. Father had no such advantage and so asked the salesman to show him clutch, brake, accelerator and gears. After five minutes of fast talking he made the sporting offer of starting the engine so Father could drive out of the showroom.

Twin and I were waiting on the corner to watch the exciting new advent of the new occupant to the freshly painted asbestos garage at the end of our narrow drive. Unfortunately, in the excitement I had forgotten to remove my scooter from the concrete strip and a pale-faced and sweaty father fumbled for the handbrake as we rushed ahead to save the scooter from this rakish sports saloon. We were too late and had to leap on to the lawn as he crunched over my pride and joy, only to drive straight through the far end of the garage. The dislodged water-butt, as it up-ended, provided enough restraint to stall the engine.

Mother's look of proud ownership of such an unusual status symbol rapidly faded to concern as the garage rocked expensively against water-butt and neighbour's fence.

"Shall I put the kettle on?" said she, without waiting for a reply.

"Wretched boy," grumbled Father, stumping indoors, "why can't he put his scooter away?"

"Never mind," consoled Twin, "you can borrow mine sometimes. Come on, stop crying, we'd better rescue our goldfish and put him in a bucket until we can get the water-butt up and filled."

The thrill of ownership soon improved Father's demeanour towards me and the promise of a new scooter 'one day' was rashly made.

Within a few days he had mastered the control and soon began to exhibit sporty characteristics, such as changing down with many revs to save the brakes and describing the geometry of flattening a curve for fast cornering.

One Sunday morning, after an urgent telephone call, he was asked to pick up a relative at Barking Station. We were allowed to come in our bedroom slippers, because nobody would see, providing we stayed in the car. In Mother's world, the general public never saw respectable people in their slippers. Father drove very sportively, we sensed he rather enjoyed a legitimate excuse for worldliness so soon after the Plymouth Brethren's morning meeting of Breaking of Bread.

Demonstrating how to overtake trams on the inside if no passengers were alighting or swerving violently to the outside otherwise, he overdid the swerve and the battery, housed in a metal box under

*Austin Seven fabric saloon*

*Mother and Twin braving Uncle's 1926 bull-nosed Morris tourer, prone to shedding petrol cans when swerving!*

the seat, hammered through the acid corroded metal and fell into the road with a sickening sliding noise. Everything went dead: we had stopped in the middle of the tram lines. Father jumped out and raced across the road to a garage which was miraculously open Sunday lunchtime. Two men pushed the Riley into the garage, another washed away spilt acid with a watering can before kicking the fragments into the gutter. A tram appeared a few minutes afterwards and we boarded, complete with bedroom slippers. So well had the proprieties of the day been drummed into us, we were acutely embarrassed on the several trams involved in our journey home and, even worse, on the platform at Barking Station.

So tight was the motoring budget that the cost of a new battery meant several planned trips were cancelled - learnt, as usual, by overheard conversations passed on to me by expert Twin.

Metallurgy, as applied to metal engines, was not so sophisticated and engines often required re-boring at twenty to thirty thousand miles. The Riley was re-bored and Father arranged to collect the car and join us at Uncle's farm in Cobham, Kent, for lunch on Saturday. The queue for the Tilbury car ferry was very long and he decided to come via the Blackwall Tunnel and enjoy the fast (for those days) North Kent, London to Rochester road. However, the garage had not told him it was necessary to treat the engine carefully for the first hundred or so miles and, in his exuberance and also trying to make up lost time, he drove so hard that the engine seized. He finished the journey by train to Sole Street Station and a long, hot walk to the farm. Shortly afterwards he joined the A.A., regarded by him as an expensive, but prudent, luxury. It proved to be of short term benefit as the young mechanic from the local Brethren's Assembly, to whom Father lent the Riley, smashed it beyond redemption on the new fast road to Woodford when showing off to his girl friend. Insurance was expensive and Father, never completely sold on the idea and certainly under-insured as a result, never received a penny in compensation. Although Twin and I missed the car, secretly we were sure it was a fair settlement for ruining my scooter.

The garage remained empty until an uncle came to live with us and parked his ancient Fiat (two seater with dickey seat) in the drive if the engine failed when swinging into the haven or, if the doors had been left open and he had enough impetus left, inside the garage. Damp mornings, with rickety magneto, presented starting problems. Father suggested, from his superior position as an ex-owner, it might be a good idea to cover the plugs with an old raincoat at night, thus alleviating condensation problems. Uncle followed this advice to good effect until one morning when he forgot to remove the coat before using the starter motor. After screaming noises the engine strangled itself and Uncle had to cut the torn fragments of his coat from the cooling fan pulley.

That was the first car I steered, sitting on Uncle's lap, Twin leaning over his shoulder to squeeze the horn bulb when necessary. Sadly, one day in a swerving response to her message of a jay--walking cat, the lurch unseated the running-board--mounted petrol can. Uncle never bothered to use the notches provided on the cap to tighten against leakage and the petrol seeped away into the gutter by the time his brakes drew us to a gentle halt.

Most cars carried petrol cans on running-boards or rear carriers and each petrol company had its own colour: Shell was scarlet; Pratt's green; B.P. a different green; Carburine cobalt blue; and National Benzole Mixture, Father's favourite, yellow. Until the early twenties petrol was often

146

sold in two gallon cans; hand operated petrol pumps rapidly took over and frequently appeared outside village stores and blacksmiths' forges. We found their operation fascinating: a large handle at the side was moved backwards and forwards to pump petrol from the underground tank into a glass dome above the operator's head, but clearly visible to the customer. When full a tap on the hose was opened by the mechanic and gravity then fed the petrol into the car. A prominent notice suggested 'Ensure Glass is Full before Delivery' or similar words, to advertise the honesty of the proprietor in warning clients of a possible fiddle. A friend of ours, who worked in a garage, confided in Father one day that he saved the petrol left in the hose by keeping the nozzle as high as possible when moving from petrol tank to the bracket beside the pump. When the car had disappeared he recovered about $\frac{1}{4}$ pint each time, which fuelled his motorbike.

In the mid 20s a young lad beginning work in a garage was paid £1 for working from 8 am to 6 pm Monday to Friday and 8 am to 1 pm Saturday and, as petrol at its cheapest was a shilling a gallon, that modest liquid 'gleaning' was understandable and, provided that customers were not offended, no doubt tolerated by the proprietor. We had one rather frugally minded friend who made a habit of instructing the mechanic to drain the hose after filling, particularly if the car was parked rather near the pump, thus providing a deep loop.

By the early 30s Tetra-ethyl-lead was introduced in petrol to combat 'pre-ignition knocking' or 'pinking', as it became known. The Anglo American Oil Company introduced it and advertised as 'Pratt's Ethyl', depicting a petrol pump drawn to resemble a young lady (puns were still very popular between the wars). Later on, they changed the pump to a character named Tommy Prattkins; humorists soon got to work in cartoons and the name was changed to Esso!

By 1939 petrol was between one shilling and fivepence, rising to one and seven in Scotland because of delivery costs [7p to $7\frac{1}{2}$p].

Many petrol cans still exist as prized souvenirs of the leisurely days of motoring. Most were made by the Valor Company, complying with the strictly enforced law that they should be at least 20 gauge tinned steel, with brass screw cap and leather washer. The words 'Petroleum Spirit - Highly Inflammable' were to be clearly embossed. The earlier cans even had special wire seals passing through neck and cap.

Three grades were marketed: One, the best; Two, known as Taxibus Spirit; and, Three for commercial vehicles. It could be said that One and Three were roughly equivalent and forerunners of 4 and 2 star today.

Engines burnt oil in far greater quantities than today and every garage had small hand-operated pumps (without glass domes) with several grades of oil available. The more worn the engine, the thicker the oil ordered, until agricultural quality signalled a rebore of the cylinders was imminent. When electric petrol pumps began to appear, large, thirsty cars flocked to avoid the embarrassment caused by needing many gallons from the weary attendant at a hand operated pump.

One thrilling day an uncle, who had spent £80 for a second-hand 6 litre Bentley (ex-a famous brewing family who disposed of their cars to a car breaker so that nobody else would own their famous pride and joy) and who had persuaded the car breaker that he would never advertise the name of the original owner, took us for a 'spin'. The vehicle was enormous with Bedford cord upholstery, speaking tube and fabric exterior, apart from wings

148

and bonnet. It was a top gear car capable of about ten miles per gallon. The tank held over twenty gallons and, as he was down to the last few gallons, a stop had to be made at the nearest small garage. When Uncle said, "Twenty gallons, please.", the attendant double checked. After several minutes of heavy work the sweat was pouring from his forehead. My whispered enquiry to Uncle resulted in him asking if I could be allowed to work the hand pump in order to fill the Pratt's 2 gallon can on the running board. It was such hard work that I gave up halfway through.

Uncle used that magnificent machine travelling England, selling machinery until World War II, when it was requisitioned for Civil Defence ambulance work and endowed with a hideous wooden body. Driven mainly by volunteers, scared stiff by the power and often, if female, too weak to change gear on cold mornings requiring a knee jerk to shift the lever against sticky cold oil, the clutch gave out and Uncle mourned the abandoned masterpiece of motoring history rotting in a dump near Bromley.

Some motor cars between 1925 and 1939 lasted better than others. The most famous, apart from Rolls-Royce and Bentley is the ubiquitous Austin Seven, the first 'peoples' car' at affordable price and sturdy design; over 3,000 are still in use and much loved in 1991. A brilliant design to encourage men away from motorbike and draughty side-car and give women an easy car to drive, steer and stop, without getting wet and also one which would accommodate at least two small children on the back seat, it was an instant success and saved the Austin Motor Company from folding.

Austin was a well-known and respected name in the field of large saloons and tourers of 12 horse power or more and renowned for reliability with genteel style. There were many other marques equally famous; competition was fierce and money getting tighter. The Great War had broadened people's horizons and post-war roads rapidly improved, together with signposts and garage facilities; exactly the right circumstances for an astute, capable engineer-cum-salesman to exploit with the right article. Herbert (later Sir Herbert) Austin managed it better than all his competitors. The 'Baby' Austin, as it was popularly named, became the dream of all 'would-be' motorists and the reality of some, including Father, who hired an immaculate 1927 Austin Seven Fabric covered four seater (two rather cramped!) saloon from our Uncle Thomas, who proudly owned and drove a much larger Austin limousine reputed, maybe optimistically, to be able to achieve sixty miles an hour on the few suitable roads. The brotherly and, therefore modest, fee for the entire summer was only £5.

To Twin and me this was the inexpensive cost of entry into worlds unattainable by normal means of bus and train fares. So simple, straightforward and sensible was the design of Austin Sevens any-body could cope with the mechanics, including me at the age of six.

Our model had the four gallon petrol tank on the scuttle, hidden under the fabric. To fill it was necessary to open the bonnet and remove the filler cap, hoping the garage attendant would not spill petrol over the hot (generally very hot) engine. Fuel was fed by gravity to the brilliantly simple carburettor, sporting a small rod which, when lifted by hand, allowed petrol to enter the float chamber, as sealing needle under the float was lifted. When fingers were thoroughly soaked with petrol the chamber was filled. If being started by handle, an old rag was stuffed into the air intake, but on well maintained examples the wire beneath the dashboard was pulled, thus closing the brass flap (in Father's

150

case a carefully scissored cocoa tin lid) which cut off air and richened the mixture. It was vital to advance the ignition with the conveniently placed lever on the steering wheel column for starting and rapidly retard to avoid angry noises. The hand throttle linked with foot accelerator had individual whims which had to be learnt with every car.

On reflection, my father was either irresponsible or lenient or, maybe, ignorant or so well versed in Austin Seven quirks, he realised it did not matter if I was allowed to start the car for him, having checked petrol, water and oil. This I did whenever he advised we were to take a trip. While he was having his after-lunch coffee, I soon learnt there was only an eighth of an inch, or less, difference between the clutch being engaged or not, as far as the clutch pedal movement was concerned. To avoid 'bucking' down our narrow drive (during parental coffee) it was necessary to let the clutch pedal up very slowly and smoothly and, to avoid the modern tendency of slipping the clutch until the drive is taken up, it was vital, and surprisingly easy to learn, to gently, but firmly, engage the clutch before attempting to use the accelerator. In other words, the clutch was either in or out. The saloon Father hired had sufficient headroom for him to wear his bowler hat with room to spare. This model was named by the public as the Top Hat Saloon.

A friend of ours with wife and two small children bought a battered 1926 tourer, the 'pram hood' model, for £5 in order to have a holiday in Scotland. It was hugely successful and, on arriving home in Woodford, was sold for £4/10/0d.

Launched in 1922 at an announced price of £225 this was reduced on 1923 to £165 when 2,400 had been made, most in tourer ('Chummy') form. In 1930 the price was £130 and, by 1933, £105 for the cheapest two seater tourer and £128 for the de-luxe saloon. Competition was fierce, with the Ford Motor Company producing a Dagenham-built metal saloon of 8 h.p. for £100. One of our first trips to London was to witness the unveiling at Earl's Court of a black two-door saloon, which in its way became as popular as the Ford Model T.

An interesting reflection on the shrinking value of money can be seen if the Metro at £6-7,000 is regarded as the successor to the Austin Seven at £128 over 50 years ago; and insight into the nostalgic outlook in these relatively wealthy times can be gained if prices paid for good condition pre-war cars are studied. Recently a 1926 Austin Chummy changed hands at £6,000 and a 1928 Fabric Saloon at £5,000. Boats and aircraft also fetch high prices, if made between the wars, as do trade vehicles and farming implements.

One mechanical method of travel, the airship, which emerged between 1917 and 1930, has not caught the imagination of collectors, as none has survived. Twin and I saw the last just before it crashed in 1930. We were enjoying a picnic in gladed Hainault Forest when we heard droning engines overhead. The R101 sailed into view, very low and slightly crabwise. Father told us it was 777 feet long and 132 feet high, containing over five million cubic feet of highly inflammable hydrogen. Apparently it was capable of 70 m.p.h., but over Hainault it seemed to be labouring. Father said it was made at Cardington, near where he was born and that another had been built there, but broke in two over the River Humber in 1921. Possibly, he said, because it could fly at almost 20,000 feet. He seemed to disapprove of airships and aircraft in general. We had to be very circumspect when enquiring of such views unless we were ready for an erudite lecture, based on the literal interpretation of Scripture.

We were lucky on this occasion, only being

given a text from the *Epistle to the Ephesians*, Chapter 2, Verse 2. 'Wherein in time past ye walked according to the prince of the power of the air, the spirit that now worketh in the children of disobedience'. Our blank looks resulted in Father's explanation, "The prince of the power of the air is, of course, Satan, that fallen angel, and we can infer he has special power in that sphere, which he exercises freely under God's control; that is, he is permitted to exercise his power in these directions."

Twin and I wandered off into the bracken to discuss this alarming thought. Did that mean all those dashing Biggles characters in my *Boy's Own Annuals* with their flimsy bi-planes were braving not only the Hun but the devil himself? Twin thought not, "God," she observed, "is up above all that, looking down."

We then discussed the Air Show in Goodmayes Recreation Ground when a small bi-plane dropped bags of flour on the cricket pitch and the canvas Imperial Airways air liner skimmed the rooftops to land on the football field. "Do you think the pilots know about the devil up there?" queried Twin.

Conditioned by boys' books and magazines full of patriotic saviours of the nation performing incredible feats of daring, I replied, "They're brave enough not to bother." After nervous giggles, we decided it was rather a wicked thought and peered through our bracken cover to make sure parents were not within earshot.

A few hours later the R101, more than three times the length of a modern jumbo jet, en route from Cardington to India could not overcome design faults and crashed in adverse weather at Beauvais, with the loss of 48 lives, including two government ministers. The government immediately scrapped the airship programme for linking Britain with India, south-east Asia, Africa, Australia and Canada.

I had heard the news on my bedside (frowned upon) crystal set when Father produced the *Daily Mail* headlines at breakfast. My blank expression, covering up slightly guilty feelings of having prior knowledge, and a filial desire to allow Father his dramatic moment, prompted me to restrict response to, "Oh, how terrible!"

In our usual eavesdropping session we gathered nobody could expect to be protected in the domain of the devil. This view was by no means uncommon in fundamentalist Christian circles of the time.

Father broadened his outlook by his study of the Scriptures in the original languages and also under the tolerant atmosphere of the Anglican Church when he returned to the fold in middle life, so much so in fact that his first flight to the Holy Land was bravely and safely endured in an ancient Dakota. Mother told us he was putty faced and wet palmed. We all agreed, given his background and earlier views, we had a brave Father who must also have exercised a great deal of faith and earnest prayer on the trip.

*\*\*\**

Over a decade later, on another picnic at Hainault, a cycling friend and I saw hundreds of German 'planes, in awesome formation, bombing East London, wave after remorseless wave, until the sky was black with mushrooming smoke, only alleviated by occasional pathetically ineffective puffs of white defiance from our palpably inadequate anti-aircraft shell-bursts.

Barely a few moments before hearing the ominous droning of approaching bombers, we had been admiring glinting golden sunlight on the gilded cross surmounting St Paul's Cathedral dome, clearly visible from the highest point of Hainault Golf Course on such a clear day.

We feared the war was ending violently before

our horrified eyes as the capital exploded under thunderous bombardment. As we sat in stricken silence, even though only about twelve miles away, we felt earth tremors beneath us, to which the appropriately named Quaking Grass (*Briza media*) responded to stimulus from below, instead of to gentle breezes.

On a memorably solemn cycle ride home, noting people's fearful expressions, and full of foreboding ourselves, it was easier for a time, to identify with Father's interpretation of Scripture and ascribe such indiscriminate carnage to the Prince of the Power of the Air!

That fateful day, with its dramatic demonstrations of human wickedness, frailty, folly and disregard of the sanctity of life, enabled me to at least understand the apparently negative stance of conscientious objectors, of whom Father was one during the 1914/18 struggle, serving time in Birmingham prison until persuaded by a fellow Plymouth Brother to join the Army's Non-Combatant Corps for mundane (latrine) duties supporting troops at Tilbury. With that background, my compromise was to join the non-belligerent, but vitally active, Merchant Navy. The friend sharing horrors with me on that day, died in khaki in Italy.

Ilford, in common with all London suburbs, received a large share of bomb devastation, which at the time augured ill for its shape being recognisable after the war; however, with typical East London suburbanites' resilience and optimism, bomb damage was restored and life returned to normal.

Our first house after marriage was a rebuild on a bomb site in Seven Kings; building permission only being granted on that accord in view of acute shortage of materials. Wood was in particularly short supply and any available under permit was not

155

adequately seasoned. Our bay-window frames, shortly after initial varnishing, actually sprouted pale green willow leaves; we hoped a good omen for rebuilding of ruined cities and towns. Perhaps a veritable phoenix from blood-stained ashes? Except that the London suburbs, unlike the legendary Arabian bird, had not set fire to themselves!

*Mother's reflecting pince-nez, with the twins in 1923*